PROPS

---

7 OBJECTS THAT CHANGED HISTORY

NORM COADY

Copyright © 2024 by Norm Coady

All rights reserved.

No part of this book may be reproduced in any form or by any electronic or mechanical means, including information storage and retrieval systems, without written permission from the author, except for the use of brief quotations in a book review.

For Nyjier Williams

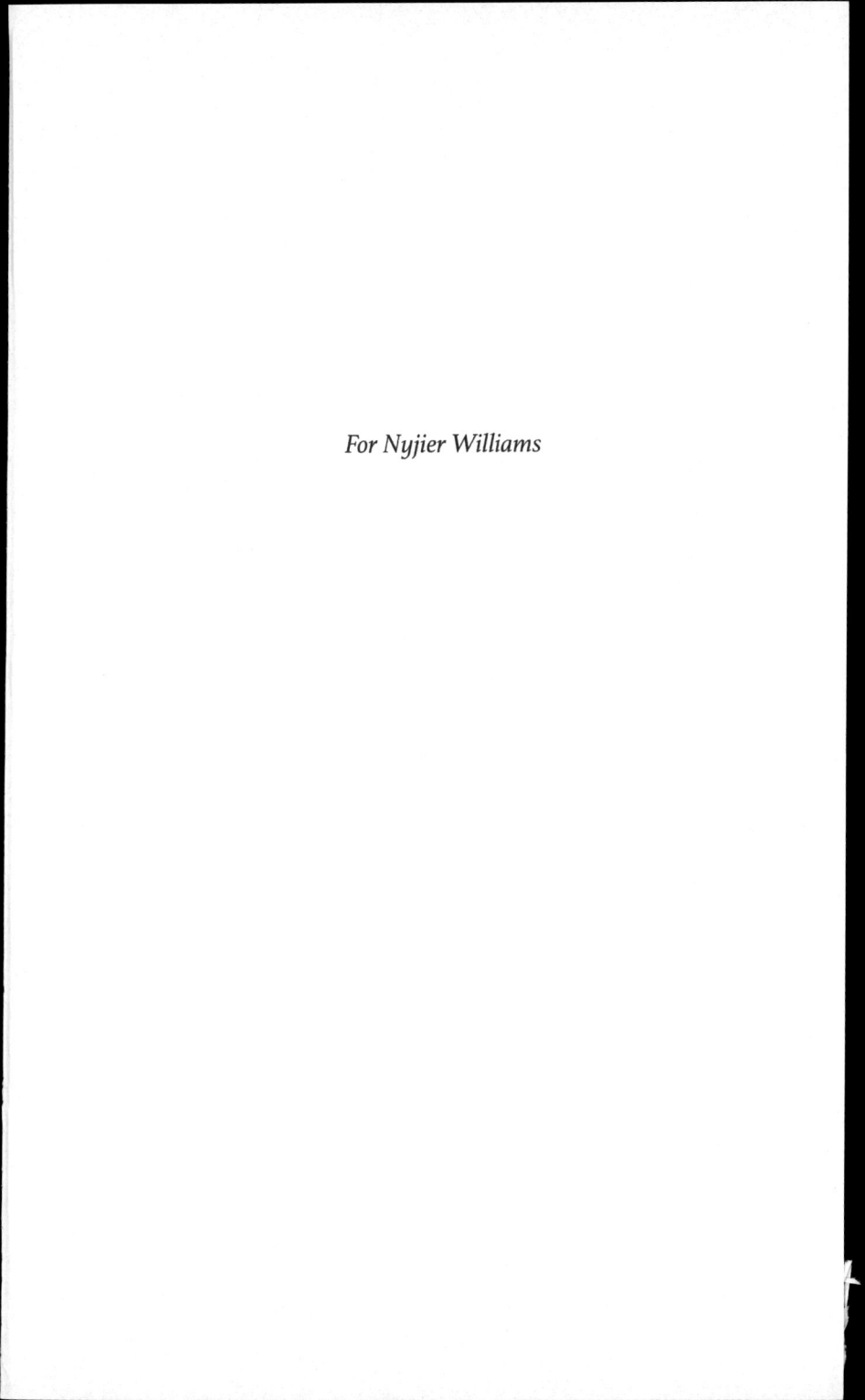

1

PAPER CUP, PART 1
JANUARY 14, 2014

The High School of Commerce in Springfield, Massachusetts is a cold, solid building built long before game-changing innovations would make standard schools like this flimsy and cheap. Even a sizable bomb wouldn't do much to it; though, many of its occupants have fantasized about the possibility. The linoleum is thick enough to be carcinogenic, and the interior walls are glossy yellow bricks. It's up on a hill, and the view, while not inspired, is not bleak.

If there's a problem with the building, it's that it is so intensely uniform on every floor of the interior, with no distinguishing marks whatsoever, that it is very hard to find your way around, especially if you're new to the place. It feels like a building designed to convince you of your own anonymity, like a prison. If you're a 14-year-old being dumped into the building for the first time, or a new teacher placed there to receive them, it feels like a shallow, disturbed sleep you cannot wake from. Not a nightmare, just a high-pitched anxiety dream for me and my young students.

And there are some nightmare touches, flashes of dysfunction I cannot forget even now, more than ten years later. Walking down a hall and having a kid with wild eyes pressed up to the window of a door, his mouth wide open, slowly sliding down, leaving a trail of mucus. Or take Nia Evans, for example, four foot ten and filled with a rage that pulsated out in almost visible waves. Picture Nia swinging a globe wildly with one hand while ripping another girl's hair out with the other. There's a chance she will bash this girl's head in with Planet Earth, the kind of fun fact that turns an object into a prop and converts a routine school beating into national news: TEEN HOSPITALIZED BY WORLD BEATER.

So, there's not a lot of time to examine the factors motivating Nia, like the fact that her dad died in a police chase last year. My career might end in the next 60 seconds. This globe needs to find a shelf before it breaks someone's head open, and there's no telling what might be involved in that process and who might get hurt trying to make sure no one gets hurt. If I'm lucky, it will only be me.

So yeah, it's that kind of school. It is separated from the outside world by thick walls as a building designed to contain and hide its citizens. The building's job – the administration's job – the teacher's job – is to make sure people outside aren't bothered by the people inside. It's a fortress of obscurity.

But right now, it's calm, and I'm out in the hall with a

paper coffee cup. This is the good time, the daily safe space. It's morning, before the first bell, and students are sleepy but friendly, milling around, throwing harmless punches, and basically, waking up together. It's a time of truce. First block and the associated hostilities have not commenced. Teachers and students can be with one another and recognize we'd likely be acquaintances, if not friends, in another life. They drive me crazy, but I like them, and they kind of get that I've been put there to make their life hard but that I'm not crazy about the role, either.

I've got a paper cup filled with coffee in my hand. *Hot* coffee. In the context of this book, it prompts a question: is this just an object, or is it also a prop? Hard to say, at least for the moment. It's kind of a fluid situation (sorry) as objects can often become props. Of course, it has a clear purpose, which is to hold coffee. Hot coffee. So, that makes it an object. But why isn't it a ceramic mug?

There's drip coffee in the faculty lounge, and I could economically tote around some affable mug advertising me as the world's best dad. But Coady can't do that. Mugs suggest plugger status, a commitment to decades of drip coffee from the faculty lounge, tenure, and a pension. No thanks. Coady is cooler than ceramics. Sometimes he wears a vest like a cowboy and boots with a bit of a heel and a pointed toe. Cause Coady is cool like that. His students may not see it that way, but it's important for Coady to see it like that; otherwise, he might find himself lost in long corridors that all look the same, unable to awaken from his disturbed sleep. So, maybe the paper cup is more than an object because there's a choice there, an attempt to signal something, a significance. It's a prop Coady uses to let everyone know he hasn't committed. He is temporary. Like a paper cup, Coady is disposable.

And here's the other thing, folks: the paper cup in my hand gives me an alternative focal point when I'm out in the hallway as the day begins. This is a practicality that goes beyond coffee. Without a paper cup in my hands, I'm simply the law in the hall. I have to pay attention to every little thing the kids are up to. I'm all eyes, no hands. With the paper cup, I can look down. I can bring it up to my lips, spin on my heels to avoid seeing something I might otherwise be mandated to report, and even uncap the cup in a pinch and give it a sniff, which doesn't exactly make sense but satisfies a need for plausible deniability.

Thank God for plausible deniability.

With a paper cup in my hand, I will never be totally at loose ends. I have a reason for existing. And vanishing. And so, I ask you: has the paper cup now passed from simply being an object into becoming a symbol? Does it qualify as one of the props in this book?

Perhaps. Maybe. Possibly.

Now, if you were one of my students dutifully sitting in a row you might wonder where all of this is going, a feeling you might want to get used to. Like so many before you, you might arch a brow and give a knowing look to your friend one row over that says, "There goes Coady again."

And you'd be right. I'm drifting off-topic, neglecting the history I get paid well to present so I can instead tilt my lance at distant windmills. After all, this is a book about history, and here I am talking about coffee inside a paper cup that is hot. By the way, that last part about the coffee being hot; it's not something you'd ordinarily have to stipulate. Coffee cup? Of course, it's hot. Does it arouse your suspicions? I hope so.

But let me be clear about one thing: the ensuing chapters don't have titles like "Deodorant Stick" and "Stapler." This is not a memoir. We'll hit the real history shortly. But first, I'd like to argue that this scene from my personal history isn't so different from the "real" history we'll be cavorting with soon. The drama surrounding this paper cup will have echoes in the chapters that follow. Yes, this tale is less deadly and lacks the historical weight of the others, but it may be just as complex, and it will have consequences of a kind. Your story, my story, Caesar's story, they are not so different. And if objects are a way of understanding history, then let's take a moment and acknowledge that our lives are filled with props.

Remember being 11 and buying the leather racing gloves that were going to turn around your social life? A prop. Did they give you the sense of belonging you longed for, did they pass by largely unnoticed, or did they lead someplace unexpected? How about your trademark oversized sunglasses with the light tint you used to wear at night in Brooklyn? Quite a dicey prop, if you ask me, and one that worked only once they were removed. And what about the white suit, the box with a ring in it, your bicycle leaning against the railing of the Manhattan Bridge overlooking the East River: props, props, props.

And what is a prop? We all kind of know what it means, but how do we define it? In the most limited sense, it's short for property, and it's those objects on the set that the actors can actively engage (gun) or we, as viewers, passively absorb (a well-worn couch).

But as this is not a book about a film set, it's a book about history, so I'd like to suggest an alternative definition for a prop. For our purposes, a prop is an object that takes on symbolic significance beyond its intended purpose. It is a catalyst or a sponge or an excuse or a diversion. Plus, there needs to be something false about it precisely because we are talking about so-called real life and not a play or a film. And for something to be false, its use cannot be too certain, at least at that moment we're looking at it. It may have a specific purpose most of the time, but at the moment we view it, it must transcend this purpose or be repurposed somehow.

So, what about the paper cup of coffee in my hands? By this point, hopefully, you're wondering what's going to happen to the hot coffee inside of it. And if you wonder about this long enough, all of a sudden you are six pages deep in this book. Well, I will tell you this: the paper cup is a prop but not an interesting one. Not yet anyway.

Someone else will have to work that magic.

. . .

I'M in the hall by my classroom with a paper cup filled with hot coffee. There's a group of boys in the near distance. I see them. These are the middle crew, the morning warm-up crew. None of them are bad, but they don't behave in class and could easily be led astray.

The "good" kids, the straight arrows, aren't on the scene yet because they time their entrance into school for minimal exposure to the cauldron – passing through metal detectors in the basement after the crowd thins to a trickle, up the anonymous staircases that all look the same, and then through the door and to their desk moments before the bells rings: seven hours of survival to go. They are resilient in ways the Navy Seals might want to study.

There's another crowd that's also notably absent, though for other reasons. The tough kids who are part of a network of spontaneous intelligence, a world of subterfuge and drug dealings and muscle that moves from the toilet stalls onto the cracked pavement, down Route 91 at high speeds into the outer boroughs of New York City, and onto ships coming in from China with all kinds of dangerous lures for America. The Navy Seals might also be inclined to study these students, though for different reasons. Armando (I have changed all the names of people at the High School of Commerce for the sake of their privacy) is part of that crew, and he never partakes in the morning glow. Years later, he'll stab a cop then chase that same cop down the street and get shot dead. Mateo is not part of the morning routine, either.

He'll eventually be sent to prison for life for gunning down another driver on the highway.

The morning crew kids in front of me now, as I sip my hot coffee, are basically that: kids. They're not good in school, they will test your patience, but they're not looking for real trouble, nor could they keep up with it if they found any. Of them all, only Andre is close to slipping into the hard crew. The rumor is that last week they gave him weed to sell, but that he screwed it up and flushed it down a toilet in a panic, making a big, sweet-smelling mess in the bathroom. But it's just a rumor. Whatever the case, he's back here with the morning warm-up team, demoted to the minors, and happy to be throwing fake punches instead of real ones.

So happy, in fact, that he's beginning to move toward me. I'm clocking his every step, pleased he's including me in his morning rounds but also a little unsettled due to the nature of our relationship. We've butted heads for months, jousting and jesting, and I still can't figure out if he's a comic genius or has absolutely no sense of humor at all, mostly because he's really funny when he's demonstrating how unfunny he finds something. This makes him an irresistible foil for me and has led to one of the most dangerous of all phenomena in a place like this: blurred lines.

You can be at odds with a student and set really hard battle lines; that's fine. There's no room for confusion. But Andre and I don't have hard lines. We have been poking at one another loosely, cracking jokes, attempting to one-up the other, neither of us really understanding the other's full capabilities. Worse, other students are amused by our show, and that's the other most dangerous phenomenon in a place like this: an audience.

Both of these phenomena are in place, and Andre begins to close the space between us. Plus, there is a whole host of other potentially dangerous factors like the fact that I have no Block 1, so I'm at ease, not preparing for class and in a good mood. The only thing more dangerous than a bad mood here is a good mood. All kinds of mistakes happen when your guard is dropped.

He reaches me and throws a light jab and then a cross, really quite playful and easy. Of course, I have the paper cup filled with hot coffee in my hands, so it's not easy to mimic his moves, but I bring up my own dukes, do a quick head fake, and extend out. We're both smiling now, and so I drop down, take a quick step forward, and go for an uppercut, and then he is suddenly gone, spinning back around, and rejoining the other group of students.

I don't make much out of it until I hear him loudly protest, "Coady hit my foot! Coady hit my boot with his foot!" He's looking down at his boot in what I take to be mock horror. It's just his kind of humor to get that worked up about something so small. It's his schtick, right? His routine, his comic genius. Right?

I can't resist discovering what comes next, and a notion of how to turn the tables occurs to me. If that sounds stupid to you, then yes, it is. Now, it's me closing the distance between us and reaching him in a small crowd of other students – an audience – and squaring off, lightly lifting up my boot, focusing its toe and tapping Andre's boot on the snout. A smile of a different kind is on my face; the kind that says, "What do you think about that?"

And here's the interesting thing: he does think about it. What happens next might lead you to believe he isn't thinking at all, but I can see him thinking about it. There's this moment suspended in the air with Andre looking down at his disrespected boot, ever so quickly glancing left and right to the kids of the warm morning glow, and then a string of calculations racing through his mind. I am mesmerized, watching him think about this, just the two of us squared off on the stage of the anonymous hall, wondering what happens next.

OKAY, let's be clear about what we are doing here. The paper cup filled with hot coffee will just have to wait for a moment. You want serious history, you want to keep me honest about the title of the book, so let's set our terms, shall we?

Yes, terms. It's not something most authors do with their readers. Most authors you can trust or think you can trust or have been told you can trust. But I prefer that you not trust me, just as I inculcate in my students the sneaking suspicion that I am messing with them. Constantly. This fundamental distrust breeds skepticism, which keeps us sharp and very much awake whether in class, or while reading a book, and perhaps, sometimes, even at night.

This book is very much a construct. Each chapter has a prop at its center, an object from which we can better understand an event or set of factors. And it can also inform us about objects and how they are used and misused. This is done for your light entertainment, hopefully, and it is an organizing principle that gives some kind of shape to the whole. But it is, always, a construct, a schema to contain information, and let's be honest, it often goes off topic and crams a bunch of interesting information in the same set of pages while pretending it all means something and that history can be easily grasped and packaged.

I would feel bad about doing this to you if I wasn't pretty sure it's happening all the time. I can't imagine a history book that isn't a construct of one kind or another, and the idea that people think history is a real thing baffles me. I appreciate historians and their contribution to the body of knowledge, but I've read enough of it to know that it is an impossible proposition, and it is better to surrender to relativity before the first solid shell gets lobbed overhead.

This book contains a bunch of people scrambling on the face of the Earth, doing their best to survive and thrive, to manipulate and conquer, to find order and obtain grace. People like you and me with props of their own. And just as life is a deadly game of survival so is history. If it stops being interesting, it stops being true. Not false, just beside the point, and slowly, it disappears from view.

So, I want you to wonder about the hot coffee in the paper cup and why I've mentioned it so many times. And we just got to a key moment, and then I took you on a tangent, establishing the terms of the book, but mostly you want to get back to the hallway with Andre, so you'll likely accept almost anything I say. Perhaps you've already skipped over this or are, right now, breathing through your nose in a labored way, wondering why I keep messing with you. Good question.

But look: here's a few things I can promise you, if for no other reason than to keep us from falling into a vortex. With each prop, I will do my best to maintain some integrity within our venture. I will make sure the object chosen is, in fact, a prop. So, for example, I'd like to write about the advent of the bit and bridle as it ushered in a new level of warfare and would make for an easy chapter. But its fundamental usefulness keeps it from becoming something false like a prop. Or maybe there was some special moment when it became a prop, but I haven't found it, and I'm not going to include it in this book. So, in this way, you can rest assured I am playing by some sort of loose rules. Good for you, good for me.

I have but one caveat: one of these chapters will have an object that does not reach the status of being a prop. Just one. Why? I would like you to be thinking, and guessing, which one of the chapters that might be. That way we are defining what a prop means in this book mostly by its presence, but also, at least once, by its absence. If we know what a prop in this book is not, we better understand the other objects that are. And suddenly, voilà, even that, too, becomes a prop of a kind. Magically transformed. Just like my paper cup.

. . .

YES, that paper cup. It's the thing between Andre and me at the moment. I've daintily tapped his boot with my boot, and I'm aware of a boundary, a blurred line, being crossed. But it is irresistible, somehow. The air leaves the hall, and everything darkens. The spotlight is on me and Andre, whose mouth is wide open and whose eyes are darting down to his foot and then left and right at the audience, and he's processing, clinically processing, figuring out what to do next. I'm watching him do this, and it's almost as if we're partners at this moment, two scientists hovering over a formula to be conjured. Teammates.

And then WHAM!!! Andre smacks the paper cup out of my hand, and the hot coffee goes EVERYWHERE, though mostly on me. I'd say the action came quickly, but I'd watched him reach this conclusion step by step.

For the kids around us, the warm-up crew, this is a bona fide stunner. They reel back, eyes widening, and emit a collective WHOOOOOAHHH!!! These are kids who usually like to feign shock and willingly stir the pot, but now their stupefaction is pure. The paper cup's lifeless, empty husk has skidded to a stop on the thick linoleum. The cup holder is down like a pair of dropped pants, and the plastic cap has rolled across the hall.

And then...well, folks, the paper cup will just have to wait. We will return to the linoleum hall and hot coffee in another chapter, *Paper Cup, Part 2*. But now our time is brief, and if we have any hope of tackling Caesar and Luther, Robespierre and Lenin, then we need to get a move on and tackle history.

So, follow me. Step up the short flight of stairs; let us tread the boards together. Our stage is littered with objects – daggers and duct tape, metal boxes and burlap sacks. Chalk drawings on the floor serve as blockings, an opened umbrella in the wings is an ominous sign. Strangely, the smell of rotten mangoes and melting wax permeates, but we know not why.

Our journey will transport us in time and then swing around and return us to the now, a supersonic round trip to February 15, 44 B.C., and back. First-rate thespians wait in the wings, dressed in topcoats and togas, robes and camouflage. They await their star turn, listening for the whoosh of the curtain and the hum of the spotlight. Someone, and I can't for the life of me remember who, said that all the world's a stage, and though it is an awfully slow-moving play, as we shall see, I am inclined to believe them.

So, with that in mind, let us recall the words of another writer whose grip on history was light but oh-so illuminating:

Admit me Chorus to this history;
Who prologue-like your humble patience pray,
Gently to hear, kindly to judge our play.

2

DIADEM
FEBRUARY 15, 44 B.C.

It is the Festival of Lupercalia, and Mark Antony is running half-naked on the streets of Rome, enthusiastically cracking a short whip while elite women hold out their hands like penitent children waiting to take their punishment. At least, I think it's a whip. I've heard it referred to as a goatskin strap, while the Ancient Greek historian Plutarch called it a "shaggy thong." Most readers in the first century probably knew what a shaggy thong was, but I do not, and lacking a staff of researchers and being on a schedule, I defer to the maxim: *get as close as you can, guess the rest*. So, let's make it semi-official: a shaggy thong is a short whip.

Thongs and whips aside, let's take a moment to really appreciate the absurdity of this scene, of what a strange and fun place Romulus' sewer is. The second-most powerful man in Rome is dangling his own shaggy thong at full sprint while the most cultured of women line the route with hopes of being lacerated by him. Some even bare their chests while Mark Antony basically bares his genitals. It makes you wonder if Edward Gibbons was right in his claim that genteel Christianity caused Rome's collapse. Because no true Christian city would host an annual ritual this ribald, *and* it's hard to imagine a people engaging in such shenanigans being beaten by a pack of barbarians. Why? Because they're barbarians themselves, albeit with nicer chariots.

Mark Antony is a case in point. Born noble, he spends his youth running with the street gangs of the Populist Publius Clodius Pulcher, joining the Cult of Lupercal, sipping blood in dank caves to worship the she-wolf of Rome. He is fond of gambling, running up a debt that forces him to flee the country, and studying philosophy and rhetoric in Greece. I also studied these subjects, but whereas this scholarly pursuit landed me in a classroom filled with teenagers, frequently fighting off clouds of deodorant spray, it sends Antony tearing around the Mediterranean fighting Hasmoneans, taking a brief break to marry his first cousin before going to work for a distant one, Gaius Julius Caesar.

Caesar uses Antony as his political proxy in Rome while he is away vanquishing Gaul, and when Antony is attacked, Caesar gets a nice excuse to march on Rome. A civil war starts and lasts four years, and Julius Vini-Vidi-Vici his way all over the place, finally coming to rest in Rome with the designation of dictator. So yeah, Antony is kind of a wild man, and he's got the bestest, most powerfulest boss in the whole known world.

His work with the shaggy thong complete, Antony charges into the Forum. He is puffing hard from his efforts, and he comes to a halt and doubles over, his whip finally at rest, sweat dotting the stones and drying in the sun. On his belt, there is a pouch, and inside this pouch, there is an object. It is not a prop yet because it has not yet seen its audience. It needs the light of day to be transformed and work its magic, and that exposure to the elements will determine Mark Antony's future and his mentor's.

Wheezing, doubled over, he looks toward the massive speaker's rostrum and sees Caesar. Julius is looking sharp in a toga, high boots, and a long-sleeved tunic. To the casual observer, his seat might resemble a throne, but it is merely a gilded chair, the kind any wealthy and delusional Roman might buy for their man cave. His toga is purple, and that's worth noting because purple is the color of royalty. He has been given special permission by the Senate to wear the color, but clearly, he is not royal. Because, let's be honest, what kind of royalty needs permission to wear purple? It's kind of pathetic, really. There are also golden laurels resting on his head, which if you squint and are an amateur, you might mistake for a kind of a crown. But it is not a crown and were you to call it a crown, most Romans, including many friends of Caesar here in the Forum, would spit on the cobblestones contemptuously. Because despite the overwhelming power of Julius, and the powder keg of potentially renewed civil war on which he sits, this is still Republican

Rome, proud of its democracy, no matter how screwed-up, debased, and unrepresentative it has become.

Plenty of Romans milling about in the Forum have no use for a dictator, particularly ones who wear gold laurels and park their purple asses on throne-like chairs. They are from powerful families, these people of the Forum, and many have been humbled at one point or another by that man up there with the fancy boots. So, as a sweaty Mark Antony bursts into the Forum like a sitcom sidekick crashing through the front door, it would be reasonable to imagine epic envy and burning resentment might be a driving force for what is about to happen.

Antony moves toward the rostrum, swaggering in his practiced way, part Roman nobility, part barbarian, a drinker of wolf's blood. Quite a specimen! But examine him more closely. His strides are not as long as usual, and his eyes are downcast. He is not the arrogant, tedious bore we've grown to love. He seems nervous, actually. His fingers are on the pouch strapped to his belt, clutching it as if he fears it will be taken away from him.

He reaches the rostrum and mounts it, kneeling before Caesar. It is his job to bestow honors upon his boss because this is the Festival of Lupercalia, and he is a high priest and Caesar's wingman. All this is expected. Routine.

What comes next is not.

As Antony kneels before the pimped-out Caesar, sweat slick on his forehead, he reaches into that pouch attached to his belt. He has a brief speech at the ready. He has learned his lines. Actually, it is only one line, probably simplified for our attention-challenged Antony. He fingers the object in his pouch – not a prop yet because it has not yet met its audience. It is still, at this moment, entirely speculative. It will either serve its purpose or kill it. No one can be sure. It's a gamble. Both men, no doubt, must be holding their breath for what comes next. What will Rome think of this object inside Antony's pouch, the one that has not yet seen the light of day? He moves to take it out, exposing it to sunlight.

It is a miscalculation of epic proportions.

ACTUALLY, this chapter is largely a catalog of Caesar's many mistakes, and this is coming from someone who has backed Julius since sophomore seminar at the great books school, St. John's College. We read Caesar back-to-back with Cato the Younger, who was ostensibly a Roman stoic, apparently because he didn't wear shoes. In reality, for a stoic, Cato the Younger did a lot of complaining, mostly about Caesar; whereas Caesar was too busy kicking ass to care what Cato thought and really would have been happy to knock off a bottle of posca with the old man had Cato been willing.

Nearly all my classmates backed Cato, loving his principled defense of the Roman Republic and detesting Caesar's authoritarian ambitions. Only Peter Conner, a streetwise philosophy student from Chicago, joined me to defend Caesar, probably because we were both in the throes of a Nietzschean phase. As two dozen of us sat around a long table, the supermajority, including both professors, waxed poetically about Cato's integrity and honesty. Looking across the table at Peter, I saw we were thinking the same thing: so what? Who wants an honest politician? They might not lie, but that doesn't mean you'll get the truth from them.

We countered that Cato was a spoiled aristocrat riding his senatorial advantages. His talk of Republican virtues was just that: all talk. Our opponents pointed out that Caesar, too, was an elite. Yes, we agreed, he was – revolutions usually come from elites. Caesar, at least, was attempting reforms – a dictatorship in the Rome of 44 B.C. was more responsive to the needs of ordinary Romans than a Republic. If our classmates really cared about representation, they would tolerate a dictatorship over a calcified system of uncaring elites. As they were, themselves, elites – though caring ones – they were horrified and reminded us that Cato the Younger killed himself! Because he had integrity! We remained unmoved, even amused. A pair of elite anti-elites poking the hornet's nest on an autumn Tuesday night. Team Caesar holding it down in Annapolis, Maryland, 1990.

That being said, in the winter of 44 B.C., Rome finds itself at an impossible impasse, and at least half of that is Caesar's fault; though, he does not originate the problem. For that, we can thank Pompey, Caesar's co-consul and once staunch ally, who becomes increasingly wary of Caesar's success in subduing the Gauls. His jealousy and paranoia build to such an extent that he moves to indict Caesar, putting him in an impossible bind. Through the Senate, he strips Caesar of his command and orders him to return to Rome to stand trial.

Now, I ask you, would you do that? No, I didn't think so.

Instead, Caesar marches on Rome with an army, sparking a civil war lasting five years, pitting cousin against cousin and turning the Mediterranean into a mosh pit. Caesar slaughters his way to the top, vanquishing opponents and becoming the dictator of Rome. A lot of people have died, but otherwise, life is good.

Then, Caesar goes and does something really, really dumb. Just idiotic. Like, "What the hell were you thinking, Jules?!" What does he do? He pardons his enemies. All the powerful people he's been fighting for years are given a free pass. He even tries to pardon Pompey, but Pompey is not having it. He flees to Egypt to rebuild; though, he is assassinated seconds after he steps on shore. Actually, he may not even reach the shore, his corpse riding the tides. Cato the Younger also eludes the sickly embrace of Caesar's pardon by killing himself. Actually, his first attempt is unsuccessful. His friends have him stitched up, but as soon as he's left alone, Cato yanks the stitches out and dies. Legitimately stoic, I must say. And it really bums Caesar out — he was looking forward to letting cranky Cato off the hook.

In Latin, these pardons are called clementia, which sounds like a venereal disease, and in Caesar's case, it kind of is. He derives a lot of pleasure in giving good clemency, a near orgasmic high in the moment of his magnanimity, but it plants the seed of a disease that will ultimately bring him down.

He forgives the orator Cicero, who will use his sharp tongue to cut up Caesar behind the scenes. He pardons cunning Cassius, who will organize his demise. He excuses Brutus, who many Romans speculate might be Caesar's illegitimate son. They are all part of a group known as the Optimates, which means the "Best Ones," an obnoxious classification, especially when applying it to oneself (which is why the obnoxious, popular kids do it so often).

As Caesar takes on the role of dictator, these Optimates vie for control of the Senate, covertly and overtly campaigning for a return to the Republic, praising Caesar through gritted teeth with fake smiles plastered on their resentful faces. They have been pardoned, and they live. And living is great considering the alternatives, but they have also been humbled. Debased, even. The fact that Cato did the "right thing" and ripped out his stitches rather than accept a pardon only makes it worse for everyone else who took one. In some ways, Caesar's clementia invites them to live in a world of unending disease. Caesar is of them, but now distinctly apart, and his magnanimity is a painful reminder of their defeat. Having conquered his own kind, Caesar has outgrown his own class, which means he's outgrown the entire system and is breaking it in the process.

And this is Caesar's problem. He can have all the power in the world, but it will not protect him from those who can get within arm's reach. Just the opposite. The more power he has, the bigger a target he becomes, and the more certain arms will want to reach out for him with pointy objects. Nor can he have less power, lest his rivals sense his weakness and strike.

So, he finds himself in a Catch-22. Damned if he does, damned if he does not. He is named Dictator in Perpetuity, due to begin on March 18th, the same day he is slated to leave Rome on a campaign. But this distinction of perpetuity only covers a living Caesar, not a dead one. Let's be honest, "perpetuity" tempts the opposite: impermanence, transience, assassination. So, even before his official designation begins, he must unofficially carry another one on his back: Target in Perpetuity.

There is, however, a fix for this issue.

A DIADEM. It is kind of like a crown if someone created a sporty version designed for practical use. As you may or may not know, playing tennis in a full crown leads to awkward turns and will cost you points. Also, have you ever tried serving in a crown? A diadem, on the other hand, is more like a royal headband. While it's not as impressive, it is more functional. Though, it would be a mistake to think its gold could wick sweat away as you make your backhand reach.

If your diadem were made of ribbon, you might be good, but usually, they resemble an oversized, bejeweled bracelet. Unless they're made of blue beads and ceramics and actually resemble a wig. Or are decorated with elephant gods and have gold bangles hanging down over the eyebrow. In fact, whereas we can all conjure a textbook crown, diadems have a wide range of models from the basic to the intricate. What they have in common is a certain understated quality. A full crown is an obnoxious limousine; a diadem is a dignified, bulletproof Bentley.

Yes, bulletproof. The understated diadem aspires to be bulletproof or at least discreet enough not to be a primary target. After all, it's risky to carry around a bunch of valuable metal and assorted gemstones on top of your head. For one, the invitation to commit violent larceny directly abuts your cranial matter, and two, you run the risk of others asking you the inevitable: *How come you got a crown on your head, and I don't?* That's actually kind of a hard question to answer, and one usually hopes that the splendor of the crown itself might cow the questioner in question. Or, I suppose, you can just have the person asking the question killed.

Now, jewels and gold are cool things to wear on your head, but that is not what makes a diadem useful. Its real value is that it is an heirloom. You can get it passed to you, and you can pass it along. A dictator is only as good as their last breath, but a diadem-wearing king has a designated successor. King dies, kid gets the crown, and now, voilà! The kid is king, ready to have kids of their own.

Yes, heirs can be of varied quality and not always the most deserving of leadership. But the roles are clear, at least. Even better, rebellion is de-incentivized when there is little chance to take power afterward. This stability is mostly worth the annoyance of the charade, as is later in history during the period of Divine Right of Rule when the guidelines really strained credibility.

People: Who put you in charge?
King or Queen: God put me in charge.
People: God? Wait, how do you know that?
King or Queen: Um...
People: Oh, whatever. I don't care. You be in charge.

Yes, it's hard to imagine God personally conveying the royal selection to mankind, especially when there are multiple popes trying to conference with him. On the other hand, we can all agree that God likes it when we're not slaughtering each other, right? This is why monarchies have been the model for a majority of civilizations – why monarchs march around with a bunch of valuable crap on their heads – and why, on balance, the vast majority of people have not challenged the fact that those valuable hats rest on someone else's head.

Besides, let's be honest, who in their right mind wants to be king?

IT IS mid-January of 44 B.C., and Caesar sits in front of the Temple of Goddess Venus. A large number of well-dressed senators approach, a group of common Romans following closely behind. They've come to present Caesar with honors. Some are heartfelt while others have been added by his opponents to satirize the entire enterprise.

When they arrive, Caesar remains seated, a move any

etiquette coach would recommend against when receiving senatorial honors in front of the Temple of Venus. Caesar dryly replies that he finds the list of honors a tad excessive for his taste, as if he is a connoisseur of honors (he is, after all), disdainful of the bouquet of praise in the obsequious snifter offered to him.

The whole ceremony highlights Caesar's awkward position. Outside of his unwillingness to kill his close friends and relatives, he is no fool. He knows there are senators for him and senators against him, and that all these sweet offerings are laced with bitters, maybe even poison. So, it becomes increasingly hard to even accept praise.

His case of clementia is spreading, impacting his judgment, making him paranoid. Caesar is best when the battle lines are clear, but now he has smudged them beyond recognition and can't find his footing. For all the talk of conspiracies against Caesar, we might be better to look at this form of self-sabotage.

Et tu, Brute?

Me? What about you, Caesar?

Shortly thereafter, there's an incident with a statue of Caesar.

Um, yes, check this out: apparently, there are statues of Caesar scattered about town, more evidence of the prop-crazy Romans. Personally, I find statues to be banality-made flesh – *hey, look, a frozen human, they must have been important; let's look at them.* For all sculptors out there laboring hard to perfect my trademark eighthead, please stop. If society needs to honor me, consider just renaming Fenway Park. I am particularly disinclined to have a statue displayed of me while I am alive. I have no interest in contemplating the contours of my own ass, and I fear the graffiti this object might invite. No good can come of this.

Caesar realizes this too late when someone places a ribbon on the head of a statue carved in his likeness. It's the simplest of diadems, embroidered ribbon, but the implication is clear: this frozen Caesar should really be a Rex.

This is the problem with symbols: they're highly symbolic. We do what we can to fix their meaning, chiseling them in marble, so they stay put. But all of a sudden, a ribbon appears on a stone head, and you've got a crisis of optics on your hands.

The situation grows more complicated when it is revealed that two Tribunes of the Plebs removed the ribbon diadem from the statue, claiming Caesar has no need for the honor. Caesar detects an element of snark in their declaration and also suspects the Tribunes were the ones who put the diadem on the statue in the first place specifically so that they could remove it. Or, who knows, maybe Caesar had the diadem placed there to see how people might respond to it. And then, these Tribunes swoop in and ruin his chance. Or maybe some Roman woman was fixing one of her sandals and absent-mindedly placed the piece of ribbon in her hand on the closest object, which happened to be the marble head of Caesar. All we know for sure is that we'll never know for sure.

But we can be pretty sure Caesar is pissed at this point

because he orders the Tribunes to be put to death, which seems a bit heavy-handed for removing a ribbon from a statue. He settles for their removal as Tribunes.

However, it doesn't look good, as the Tribunes represent the Plebs, part of his core support. It both appears weak while also actually being weak. That is to say, Caesar's overreaction to the episode hints at his fundamental insecurity, while his willingness to accept a lesser punishment for the tribunes makes him appear more insecure still. He is nosediving. He needs to find a way out of this death spiral.

WHICH BRINGS us back to where we began. It is February 15, the Festival of Lupercalia, and Antony has shaggy-thonged his way into the Forum, where a purple Caesar sits at center stage on a platform. Striding forward, though a little haltingly, Marc Antony makes his way to the center to bestow honors upon Caesar. All of this is part of the plan. What happens next may or may not be.

On bent knee before Caesar, sweating in the sun, all eyes on him, Antony reaches into the pouch strapped to his belt and pulls it out: a diadem. We have no record of what it looks like, but let's imagine it's a simple affair, very much like a giant bracelet composed of gold squares and inlaid jewels. For Caesar, one of the richest men in history, it's not the bling that sings to him. He would be just as happy with a ribbon, so long as it does the trick.

It glows with reflected light from the Sun as it moves

toward Caesar's head. Antony announces stiffly, "The people give this to you through me," and places it on Caesar's head.

Just like that. For all the purple togas and gilded chairs and ribbons on statues, the whispers and conspiracies and sarcastic honors, all it takes is a sweaty Marc Antony to change the entire calculus.

Only he doesn't. Or *it*, the diadem, doesn't. It is only a prop for a fleeting moment, the time between leaving Antony's pouch and landing on Caesar's head. It shines in the sunlight as it is being lifted but then immediately dims as it lands on Caesar. The crowd, too, dims. And sniffs dismissively. A few onlookers applaud the diadem on Caesar's head, but this mild enthusiasm only highlights the general lack of support for the display. The vast majority of hands in the Forum remain decidedly at rest. Rome does not approve.

Caesar, a pro at reading the room, removes the diadem and hands it back to Antony quickly, perhaps hoping he will stuff it back in his pouch, and it will go unnoticed. Antony is confused by this and feebly tries again, bringing the diadem back to a dejected and embarrassed Caesar. So very awkward. One can feel the strange chemistry between the two men. Are they at odds, or are they in league with one another? Is Caesar throwing his accomplice under the bus? Is he frustrated that Antony is not reading the room, too? They may have scripted the first part but not anticipated the second, and now they are fumbling painfully.

"Jupiter alone of the Romans is king," announces Caesar, a nice piece of improvisation and a sentiment that gets an appreciative round of clapping that must nonetheless have grated upon the dejected non-king.

And then the strange moment is over as fast as it began. It is like a summer squall that provides for a momentary diversion but does not actually break the terrible heat. One imagines everyone, Caesar and Antony included, thinking to themselves, "What the hell was that?" But since everyone is in public in the Forum, no one can actually ask the question, saving it for later when they might savor the possibilities in a reclined position, mug of wine in hand.

Two thousand years have passed, and we still don't really know; though, we can enjoy a glass of setinum while contemplating it. We may actually get drunk trying to figure it out because Roman records are frustratingly spotty. For an empire so old, we generally know quite a bit about it, yet key moments, reactions, and reasonings are stubbornly missing. It is like watching a highly produced movie that has 20 seconds cut from every minute at random. The space in between speaks volumes and writes them, too, as historians from every subsequent civilization speculate on what the main players might have been thinking.

Some historians believe Antony was trying to flatter Caesar. Others believe he was trying to embarrass him, while still others say Antony was trying to forcibly sober the dictator, to once and for all force him to publicly reject the idea of kingship. My own sneaking suspicion is that Caesar put Antony up to it.

Yet, we do not know for sure.

What we do know is that the Romans let Antony and Caesar know what they thought of the prop, which was very little. The diadem Caesar sought was indeed his, but only for a few seconds before he was compelled to remove it. It is a special kind of disgrace to be forced to publicly spurn what you want most and have the crowd applaud your acceptance of their rejection. Poor Caesar.

This is more than a small setback. It returns Rome to a potentially explosive status quo with a resistant Senate filled with emasculated Optimates on one side and a dictator who longs for permanent power on the other. It's not the power grab itself that might so offend many Romans as the way it presents in this case: a shallow canard engineered by Caesar, clumsily executed, and feebly covered up. You can abuse a Roman, you can flaunt your wealth and make them feel small, but you do not patronize a Roman. They do not miss much or easily forget. They will see right through you and hate you for it.

Caesar is in trouble.

CAESAR SACRIFICES a bull later that same day, but mostly, he's going through the motions. You know, it's just another Monday for Caesar: slip on the high boots, don the purple tunic, spurn a diadem, slaughter a bull. His high-priced soothsayer, Spurinna (kind of a know-it-all prick, really), reads the entrails and the message is clear – the bull has no heart, which is hard to read as anything but troubling if, for no other reason, than that it is impossible. No way can a live bull be heartless. Did Spurinna discreetly dispose of it? And why? Maybe he wants Caesar to cool it, hinting that he should not attempt an overthrow of the Republic for a Rexship. *Leave well enough alone, Jules, baby.* Caesar sacrifices another bull to try to get a better reading, but this one lacks a lobe on its liver. So, either we've randomly hit a disturbingly bad batch of bulls, or the portends are bad.

Spurinna warns Caesar of danger in the next 30 days. He does not explicitly mention the Ides of March, but it is within this range. Caesar is skeptical about omens. However, at the same time, Spurinna is highly connected, a hearer of whispers, a man whose breath can still commingle with others. For this reason, Caesar is inclined to heed his gibberish. In the mess of entrails and missing hearts, there might be a warning worth heeding. In any event, Caesar doesn't need blood and guts to know he's on shaky ground. His departure from Rome approaches, and his dictatorship in perpetuity is soon to be granted.

Other bad tidings abound. According to Barry Strauss' excellent *The Death of Caesar, The Story of History's Most Famous Assassination*, birds become strangely aggressive, odd lights fill the sky, men catch on fire spontaneously, and one of Caesar's prized horses stops eating and begins crying uncontrollably. How any of that can be verified is a mystery to me, but if nothing else, things are clearly getting tense. The month following February 15 is a stretch of awkward pauses and corners and whispers.

We see Caesar in limbo, welcomed into the best homes and subjected to awkward feasts. He is feted, but it feels kind of like he is being fattened up for the finale. The diadem episode is on many minds and many tongues. Caesar – or Antony – or the pair – made their lunge for royalty, and it failed. But what now?

On March 15, Caesar awakens to find his wife Calpurnia inconsolable. She's had a nightmare of holding a dead Caesar in her arms. She begs him not to leave for the Senate. Caesar dismisses her nightmare as troubled sleep, not prophecy, but it unnerves him. For all the years Caesar spent out of Rome, Calpurnia was very much in it. He would do well to trust her intuitions or even wonder if she knows something she cannot reveal. Caesar might not believe in nightmares as prophecy the same way he might not believe in reading entrails, but the people around him, those who rely on him for their existence, are freaking out, and that's freaking him out. Some sources claim he himself had a dream the night before, flying above the clouds, shaking the hand of Jupiter. He may have even had an undetected epileptic seizure, leaving him shaken. Literally.

Caesar runs an errand and happens to see Spurinna. With confidence, Caesar announces that the Ides of March have come, and here he is, still intact. Spurinna, like a jerk, retorts, "Aye, they have come but not gone."

It must have spooked Caesar because he elects to stay home, sending Marc Antony to dismiss the Senate. For whatever reasons, this is slow to happen, and the Senate meets anyway, the conspirators therein, their daggers – or pugio, as they are known in Rome – strapped to hips beneath their togas. With no sign of Caesar, they grow anxious. Decimus, a conspirator and a close friend of Caesar's, is sent to woo him over to the Senate. He extracts Caesar out of the clutches of his terrified wife through the time-honored practice of impugning his manhood, saying, "Will someone of your stature pay attention to the dreams of a woman and the omens of foolish men?"

This, too, is part of history, my friends. We imagine notable events are inevitable, but they hinge on an impossible number of decisions and random factors. What if Caesar had seen through Decimus' man-shaming and instead trusted his own gut? Well, for one, his gut would have stayed intact, at least that day.

The rest, as they say, is history. We are not too concerned with Caesar's actual death for our book; though, it is notable that Marc Antony is not in the Senate when his mentor meets his maker. Instead, he has been detained outside by someone seeking his council. This is quite convenient for him, maybe even suspiciously so. In any case, he hears the commotion when it comes.

Caesar is held down by his toga and Casca, a capable killer and friend of Caesar's, draws out his dagger and makes his thrust, missing Caesar's neck and hitting him in the chest. He is followed by Cassius, who slashes Caesar's face but misses with his second attempt, hitting Brutus' hand instead. And then Brutus. Yes, Brutus...

Brutus lunges forward now, landing his dagger in Caesar's thigh close to his loins, which some speculate is the origin of Brutus himself. And then, according to a fairly well-regarded dramatist, who has a tendency to play fast and loose with the truth, Caesar stands, looks at Brutus searchingly, and says...

No, he doesn't. He doesn't say, "Et tu, Brute?"

He may – *may* – have said, "Kai su, teknon," which translates to, "You too, child?" And this may – *may* - have been his attempt to reveal at the end Brutus' true lineage as his son, damning him for all time as a fratricidal goon. But even this is unlikely. These words are probably an invention of the melodramatic Renaissance. Most likely, Caesar said nothing coherent, which is consistent with the behavior of people being stabbed multiple times. Credible reports have him dropping to the ground, attempting to cover himself with his toga, and shivering.

But what fun is this? How do you stage it? How do you know when the scene is over, how the assembled actors should respond, and what Caesar thinks at the moment of his demise? Really, it's just awkward, which it must have been, in reality, awkward and awful. We paid for these seats, and we need something to talk about once the curtain falls, and for this to happen, we need a foil, we need a villain, we need a revelation, a connection, a prop.

A prop like Marcus Junius Brutus, a prominent young Roman but also kind of a blank slate, anonymous enough to allow for the enlightenment we seek. Yes, Brutus, so pliant in life, so useful in the afterlife.

Dante Alighieri, perhaps history's greatest practitioner of wielding people like props, places Brutus in the deepest icy depths of his inferno for his betrayal of Caesar. Shakespeare, who knows a thing or two about props, gives Brutus more airtime than the subject of his play, Julius Caesar. The Bard is not interested in a winner like Caesar. He likes complicated characters – then crushes them into dust. Thanks to these masters, Brutus stews in a pot with Lucifer, Judas, and whoever else is the turncoat du jour. He is the Traitor in Perpetuity.

In reality, Brutus is less of a traitor than he is a fence sitter, and for one of history's greatest villains, he's very bland fare. He had been an ally of Caesar's one-time friend, then frenemy, then full-on enemy Pompey, switching to Caesar's side when the only other positions left were death or exile. He is one of those pale, bookish Optimates that Caesar so distrusts. Though, he's not above locking five Cyprian Councilmen in a room until they starve to death. Their crime? Failure to pay back a loan with a 48% interest rate. So, yeah, that's pretty cool.

In his defense, Brutus is also a true Republican and rumored to be Caesar's illegitimate son. Probably not but possibly. So, while Brutus' heart beats to preserve the Republic, his head knows this defense may include the death of his maybe-father. Even in the ethical sewer of Rome, you're not supposed to kill your pops. Adding to his woes, he is a descendant of Lucius Junius, killer of kings and founder of the Roman Republic. This gives Brutus the kind of gravitas that makes him an attractive conspirator for Cassius, who eagerly recruits him. Brutus lends the conspiracy legitimacy, making the murder of Caesar an act of courage and idealism, as opposed to a savage pack of dagger-waving vipers piling on a single man. So, if not a prop, let's say Brutus is something of a tool.

The reality is that betrayal can be found everywhere. Dozens of daggers got within striking distance of Caesar on the Ides of March with many more giving the cabal a wide berth. If you're looking for traitors, consider Decimus, one of Caesar's most trusted friends. Not only did he join the conspiracy, but he also shamed his friend into leaving his distraught wife and heading to the Senate to be slaughtered. That's cold.

How about Marc Antony? He had been approached a year earlier about eliminating Caesar. He declined to join the conspiracy but notably failed to report it to his boss. Additionally, on the day of the assassination, Antony is prevented from entering the Senate. Did Antony somehow know, even subconsciously, that a conspiracy was afoot, deciding it was better to be distracted and far from the Senate floor? Add these sins of omission to his many other sins of inclusion.

For Antony, the party is over.

. . .

As this is Rome, any number of props could have served as the inspiration for this chapter. We could have called it *Shaggy Thongs*, focusing on Mark Antony, which would have sent the passage in a whole different direction. We wouldn't be talking about the benefits of royalty and the pitfalls of forgiveness. Instead, we might be looking at the rituals of Rome and how their pagan beliefs shaped their political order. We could have elected to call this chapter *Entrails*, and in this case, we could dig deeper to discover who Spurinna was and examine how places like Rome, so very tightly wound, deal with an uncertain future. (Not to mention diving deeper into the mysteries of the missing bull organs.)

Originally, the name of this chapter was going to be *Pugio*, a Roman dagger. After the fatal incision on Caesar, which is likely the second, the daggers go from being an instrument of death to a symbol of inclusion, of shared responsibility, of conspiracy. Grotesque as it is, these redundant dagger thrusts are essential to establishing a faction. The extra knife wounds are the equivalent of the signing of the Declaration of Independence. In for a penny, in for a pound.

Caesar's funeral is really a splendid affair, positively teeming with props. Lots and lots of props and torchlit processions, Caesar's stained toga on a spear along with other props aplenty, including beeswax mask likenesses of Caesar. Because get this: apparently, prominent Romans had waxen masks of themselves made on a regular basis in anticipation of their death. Imagine fitting that into your busy schedule.

Sorry, I can't meet you at the Forum this afternoon. I need to sit for my annual waxen death mask in case I die this year.

Caesar, never one to miss out on an honor, no matter how macabre, had masks cast. His funeral has multiple actors, trained to walk like the great man, presenting for the crowd a fair imitation of Caesar, which is one of many things that might have brought tears to Roman eyes and rage to Roman hearts.

Marc Antony gives a speech drifting up and down the scale from basso profundo grief to shrill soprano outrage. It's a real ham-fisted performance. Prior to the funeral, he brokered a peace of a kind whereby Caesar's reforms would continue in exchange for an amnesty for those involved in the conspiracy. And so, they – Optimates like Brutus and Cassius – are present at the funeral of their victim, holding their breath. But then, in true Antonian fashion, his speech inflames the crowd, which elicits the protests of the conspirators. Antony briefly walks back his comments until he further inflames them, inviting the crowd to list Caesar's great deeds. Basically, he's all over the place and crowdsources the outrage to keep the good times going. For the Optimates involved in the conspiracy, it is an increasingly tense affair.

It really gets bad when a wax statue of Caesar with dagger wounds is borne aloft by a mechanical device and rotated like a rotisserie chicken for all the crowd to behold. All of which makes Caesar's funeral sound like a cross between Burning Man and Disneyland. Predictably, people go bananas. The crowd grabs torches, attempting to burn down the houses of

Brutus and Cassius; though, instead they accidentally decapitate one of the tribunes in a case of mistaken identity.

Oh, well.

Caesar's funeral pyre burns, smolders, then smokes but will not go out. Mourning is sustained, teeth are gnashed, and names are cursed. Then, Caesar's veterans enter the city in droves, which sends the so-called Best Ones to the hills. The Optimates lose their future at a funeral of their own making.

One wonders what ran through their heads as they ran for their lives. Did they curse Caesar, themselves, or one another? Did they know they would never see Rome again? Perhaps they began to reconsider their earlier objections to Caesar. Maybe the old man wasn't so bad, after all. Perhaps a tidy little diadem for Caesar would not have been such a hardship.

Surely, it beats being decapitated in a foreign land.

FUNDAMENTALLY, the winter of 44 B.C. presented an impasse between two forces that could not be reconciled. The Senate could not afford to lose power, while Caesar's survival depended on gaining more. Essentially, both were victims of Rome's growing pains and of an Empire that needed an Emperor but could not bring itself to clear the stage for a throne.

The Optimates, who pounced on Caesar, tugged at his toga, and voted with their daggers, made the Senate floor blush for nothing. Caesar's murder did not actually reverse their waning fortunes; in fact, their conspiracy vaporized the order they sought. And because of this, both parties were sacrificed: Caesar on the Senate floor, scores of Optimates in the empire's hinterlands – tracked down, cornered, caught, and dispatched.

If you are interested in flirting with a brain aneurysm, might I recommend reading George Friedrich Wilhelm Hegel? His name alone might give you vertigo. I've spent dozens of hours poring over his Wikipedia page detailing his views on history, but for now, I will keep it simple. Hegel believed history was a continuous struggle between what is, the thesis, the challenge to that, the antithesis, and the fusion between the two that leads to a new reality. This is the synthesis. Altogether, he called this the dialectic. When we speak of Rome in 44 B.C., the thesis is Caesar. But in pardoning his enemies and leaving them alive on the field of battle, he creates his antithesis, the challenge to his own authority. The synthesis is what comes of all of it, the new blend that will become the thesis and be challenged again by a new antithesis that is waiting to create a new synthesis. It is virtually biological, and if ever there were a fascinating petri dish of syntheses, it is Rome.

Caesar does something really stupid in keeping his opponents alive and letting them stroll freely around the forum and senate. He almost seems to be inviting them to kill him. But then his opponents do something even stupider: they actually take him up on the offer, unleashing the chaos that can only lead to a king. Or an emperor. Four centuries of them, in fact. The page has been turned; the impasse broken. Space has been cleared for the throne Rome so desperately needs. Everyone will bleed profusely in the process, but a new world order has begun.

The Republic goes into the dustbin, a victim of Caesar's last stroke of genius: the appointment of a young Augustus as his successor. Just 19 years old, he will humble the Optimates, establishing for sure who is the best one – *one*, as in a *singular* one – as in *himself*. He does not repeat Caesar's mistakes. He does not have an inexplicable sweet tooth for mercy. Maybe because he is young and has seen the rot of the Republic first-hand, he is not attached to the good old days. He plays everyone off one another until there is no one left.

Cassius somehow commits suicide *and* is beheaded, his head rolling around on a field in Phillip, an act that must have either required assistance or suggested a degree of editorial commentary after the fact. Brutus falls on his sword after a defeat, pompously engaging in a whole string of final words, from a convoluted aphorism to quoting the playwright Euripides. Did he somehow know that his own historical fate would be sealed by a playwright inventing famous last words? No, not very likely, but the notion of him dying with this prophecy on his lips might keep us in our seats until the curtain falls and keep us talking about it after the show. Decimus' end is more definitive. He is killed by a Gallic chief who mails his head to Marc Antony for him to do God knows what with.

As for Marc Antony, he does his best to fulfill Caesar's

destiny. Unfortunately for him, his very best is very much a disaster, as one might imagine from such a character. He governs like someone moving an ice tray from the sink to the freezer, leaking more water than he keeps, swearing all the while. And then, Augustus plays all sides against the other, allowing Antony to consistently take a beating as his ally until finally, almost mercifully, turning on him. He traps Antony in the sands of Egypt where he faces his final days with his lover, Cleopatra. It is very much a Romeo and Juliet ending with Marc Antony stabbing himself after mistakenly hearing she had already done so. Belatedly finding out Cleopatra is still alive, he has his friends bring him to where she's hiding, so he can die in her arms.

Et tu, Cleopatra?

Yes, love, I'm here.

And what becomes of our young Augustus? Well, he assumes the role of Emperor of Rome, but no longer going by the name of Augustus. He will now be known by one word: Caesar. Caesar is dead, long live Caesar!

IN HAPPIER TIMES, before all this mess with diadems and daggers began, Caesar (the original, not the remix) was on his way back into Rome. The Senate granted the dictator the right to return to the city on horseback, an honor typically reserved for triumphs. As usual, Caesar drew a crowd. One voice from the gathering greeted him as "Rex." Others in the crowd joined in, but then Caesar gently corrected them.

"I am Caesar, not Rex," he said.

This was a humorous retort as Rex was a common Roman last name; the same way King is a common last name in America. Unlike his cloddish behavior at the Temple of Venus or his pettiness regarding the ribbon diadem on his statue, it was a graceful moment for Gaius. Here, Caesar was at ease with the people, enjoying his popularity, and the crowd in turn appreciated his modesty. It is one of the last light-hearted moments this great man enjoyed.

For all his ambitions and victories, Julius Caesar never became Julius the Rex, an oversight his nephew fixed for him. For while Rex was a designation for a king that became a last name, Caesar was a last name that became a designation for an Emperor, surviving centuries in Rome and spreading north into the royal halls of the Kaisers and Tsars.

And if that's not a posthumous mic drop, I do not know what is.

The Festival of Lupercalia. Those are "shaggy thongs" in the runner's hands. Aside from too much clothing, a not inaccurate depiction.

Caesar in happier times, when all he had to worry about was lounging with his bros and killing Gauls. Let's be honest: who doesn't want to kill a Gaul now and again?

"Et tu, Brute?" Nah, not very likely.
Maybe "Kai Su, Teknon?" But probably not that either.
Caesar probably said nothing, which is behavior more
consistent with being stabbed 23 times.

Caesar's funeral. Mark Antony oration is all over the place.
Then a wax statue of Caesar complete with stab wounds
rises up and spins like a rotisserie chicken. It's like a cross
between Burning Man and Disneyland.
Predictably, people go bananas!

3

TORCH
MAY 4, 1521

It is 1521, folks, or maybe 1522, and we are in Wittenberg, Germany, and everything is a little bit bat-crap crazy because the Reformation has transformed from a religious revolution into a political one. One minute, there's all this awesome talk about a personal relationship with God, and the next minute peasants are more interested in their personal relationship with homicide. It's chaos and not the cool mosh-pit kind. They're destroying churches, smashing stained glass windows, and worse, killing people who don't agree with them. This leads to a brutal crackdown from the princes. Dead peasants are swinging from trees like Christmas ornaments. Big, meaty, Christmas ornaments.

It's quite unpleasant especially for Martin Luther, who kind of started the whole thing. Yes, Martin Luther. No, not Martin Luther King Jr. Martin Luther, the monk who got fed up with the Catholic Church, nailed the 95 theses to a door in

Wittenberg and changed Christianity forever. He has been hiding in a castle in Wartburg, dressed in a cool tunic, and eating thin gruel while translating the New Testament into German – real tortured genius stuff.

Then, finally, this guy named Spalatin comes and gets him. They disguise Luther as "Knight George," and he heads out into a very changed Germany. Luther's ideas have "set the world on fire," literally as much as metaphorically, and Spalatin is basically throwing the consequences back in Luther's disgusted face. Luther is down for a closer relationship with God and is willing to be a bit combative to get there, but this is different. Dead peasants are everywhere, and they do not go with the decor.

Worse, some of his old buddies are part of the problem. His pal Karlstadt, whom Luther chilled with in Wittenberg, has basically gone nuts, married a teenager, and is kicking priests around like it is a sport. There are torches all over the place and plenty of statues thrown through stained glass windows.

And then, just when things are really getting out of hand, Luther skids up on his horse, dismounting like a Jedi on meth, and in an attempt to quell the chaos, starts kicking some of his own ass on the cathedral steps. He opens with this totally boss move, grabbing a torch and brandishing it like a lightsaber.

He goes for this one guy's legs with the torch, and the guy jumps like the scarecrow in *The Wizard of Oz*. It's pretty hilarious if you play it on repeat again and again. And then, torch in hand, Luther grabs Karlstadt by his lapels with disdain while ordering other people to get buckets of water to put out the fire in the church. He tosses Karlstadt down the steps scornfully and brandishes the torch at him.

And then Karlstadt, the teenage-loving radical guy, gets all confused as to why Luther is angry. They've been friends, and Karlstadt was just doing some mass killing to achieve a closer relationship with God like he thought Luther wanted.

Now, he's up in Luther's grill, and he's like, "Hey dude, what's your problem? I'm doing all this killing for you!" But Luther gets all alpha and totally rips Karlstadt a new one, waving the torch and saying, "You think this was my work? This was never my work!" and tells Karlstadt to get out of Wittenberg before he bitch slaps him right out of town.

And then the crowd, which was supporting Karlstadt, is just super surprised to see Luther, and that stops the rioting cold. It's kind of awkward. All of a sudden, Karlstadt feels like an idiot in front of his friends. He leaves the scene doing random crap and shouting, "The people's work!" a couple of times. Total idiot, right? He even pushes a rando in the crowd for no reason and then shouts, "It's the people's work!" a few more times. Man, what a loser.

And Luther, he's just like... totally smoldering, his torch blazing brightly by his face as he watches a shamed Karlstadt scamper off the screen.

Wow, Luther. Cool as hell, right?

Then, basically, everything goes back to normal. No one kills anyone else ever again, and the Reformation wins big time, which is really cool. Plus, Luther gets a hot wife. Isn't that cool? Yes, it is.

But it's also a giant load of crap.

THIS PRECEDING passage is a description of a scene from the 2003 motion picture *Luther* written more or less as if one of my teenage students were transcribing the sequence. The film is about as academic as a candy wrapper, but it does grab your attention. It stars Las Vegas Film Critics Society Awards winner Joseph Fiennes in the aforementioned torch-wielding action scenes, capturing the teenage audience while talking about concepts like predestination and transubstantiation. For that alone, it deserves an Oscar. Might I suggest: *Best Adaptation of Boring Events into a Film That Can Be Shown in Class While the Teacher Is Shopping Online*?

A day later students may not be able to tell you much about Cardinal Cajetan and the threat of the Turks in Vienna, but they will remember the indulgences, relics, and Luther's good-looking wife. Thanks to an excellent montage sequence, reminiscent of an 80s teen movie, they will be able to recall Luther striding up to a cathedral door and dramatically hammering his 95 theses in place, followed by a few fanboys rushing the document to the printing presses. Copies proliferate, blowing up the thriving indulgence dispensary of John Tetzel, who is played by Alfred Molina, better known to my students as Otto Octavius from Spider-Man, who goes by the name Doctor Octopus. Students perk right up when they see him appear on screen, figuring Doc Ock will bring some action to the show, and you know what? He does. Molina is lots of fun as John Tetzel, who was a fun guy when he wasn't tossing people down wells or ripping off peasants.

The film was partially funded by Thrivent Financial for Lutherans, which sounds as sexy as a garter belt for men's socks. Despite this, the filmmakers of *Luther* knew what they were doing. They were tasked with making 30-plus years of Luther's life look like three while holding the attention span of teenagers and spreading the message of Luther, a task I'm sure Thrivent Financial kept a close eye on. Is it highly condensed history that takes liberties and functions basically as propaganda? I don't know, is that a rhetorical question?

At the same time, having seen it more than four dozen times, I can no longer remain complacent with its pure kitsch value. There are only so many times you can see Karlstadt blowing up and yelling, "The people's work!" before you wonder just who the hell Karlstadt really was. And did Luther really wave a torch around the cathedral steps and go all gangster on everyone? Was he really kidnapped on a desolate road in the middle of the night?

Nagging questions like these lead you to Wikipedia, then to Jstor.org, and if you are really determined, to a semi-obscure volume entitled, *Frederick the Wise, Seen and Unseen Lives of Luther's Protector*. It's not exactly the same as hopping a flight to Wittenberg and blowing dust off ancient manuscripts in search of hidden truths and maybe secret codes, but it is illuminating.

Before we commence on our journey, let me dedicate this chapter to all my former students who sat through our two-block screening of *Luther*. We had our fun and enjoyed many replays of an irate Karlstadt. But now we must go deeper. We must figure out what all this means and who tried to shape that meaning and why. Because we are adults now. It's time to put the Twizzlers away and dive into real history. Trust me, you won't be disappointed.

It's time. Let's go find that torch.

Before we do, let's recap our terms.

The subtitle of this book is *7 Objects That Changed History*. This can be read in a number of ways and should be for this book. For the preceding chapter, *Diadem*, and most of the other chapters, this refers to real objects that popped up in history and sent events into a new direction. For the paper cup chapters in this book, which are more memoir than history, the object is a catalyst for transformation.

But for this chapter, *Torch*, the subtitle must be read differently. We have our object, the torch, but we are pretty sure that it is just an invention of the filmmakers of *Luther*. It is not at all likely that Martin Luther ever waved a torch angrily in front of a crowd of rioters, and the object in question really is a prop. Literally a prop. And if is a prop, or an object, that prop has been consciously chosen to alter – or revise – history, likely for the purpose of turning a confusing jumble of back and forths, innuendos sunk in sermons, and generally passive-aggressive behavior between two middle-aged men into an action sequence that looks like a late-Medieval version of *Star Wars*.

The movie has elected to be compelling rather than strictly accurate, and it seeks a specific kind of audience, one which does not include historians whose life work is the study of the Reformation. So, if you're a historian whose life work is the study of the Reformation, you might want to skip ahead to the next chapter, *Wampum*. No good can come of your close inspection here.

But if you're a popcorn-tossing, Twizzler-munching member of the broader audience, I advise you to stick around. The torch in question does change history but only when we look back and revise events. And while that might seem underhanded and wrong, strangely enough, it suits the purposes not only of the filmmakers themselves, but also, I would contend of history, too.

For the purposes of clarity, let's just say that, whether real or metaphorical, the torch represents the dispute between two Reformation figures: Martin Luther and Andreas Karlstadt. The movie could have chosen to do a sin of omission, leaving Karlstadt out lest he muddy the narrative waters, but it does not. It wants us to wonder who Karlstadt is, maybe even force us to hop on a flight to Wittenberg and blow dust off ancient manuscripts. It spends a lot of time on a second-string character like Karlstadt because Karlstadt is a good foil, and through him, we can better understand Luther. So, as we go looking for the torch, we are conscious of what its flames are meant to illuminate: Luther, Karlstadt, and the roots and offshoots of their dispute.

WITTENBERG, Germany in 1517 is a real hotbed of dissent. Turn any muddy corner and you'll bump into a theologian working up their list of grievances against the Church. There's Philip Melanchthon working on the scraps that will become the *Augsburg Confession*, a real Reformation chart-topper. Behold Thomas Müntzer, a straight-edge radical who makes Luther look like a delinquent priest and rejects the written words for spiritual existence. Later, Müntzer organizes his own militia, does battle to try to make his pure vision of a new Christianity a reality, and gets executed for his pains.

And then, of course, there is the roguish Martin Luther, who has come to Wittenberg for doctoral studies at the University. But he's not a big shot, not yet. He's just a face in the crowd – smart, with a caustic wit, and a talented lecturer but not yet a standout solo act. Not yet. If you want to find the big shot on campus you probably are better off heading to the office of Andreas Karlstadt – yes, *that* Karlstadt – Mr. People's Work! – Chancellor of the University and mentor to the other young hooligans.

It is almost like Paris in the 20s, or New York in the late 70s, except that Wittenberg is in the middle of nowhere, and no one in the world cares what second-tier monks have to say about salvation.

As it turns out, this distance will be something of an advantage for the monks. It allows their message to remain unadulterated while putting them out of range of the Papal hammer. The same thinkers might be crushed in Rome or corrupted in Augsburg with popes and cardinals scowling over their shoulders. In Wittenberg, they can simply exist, trading licks and constructing revolutionary beats.

They seek to reform a Church that is extensively, demonstrably, and incoherently deformed. There is, of course, the embarrassing issue of indulgences, documents that advance worshippers a couple of hundred years in Purgatory for the right price. It's salvation for sale. But there are also 16-year-olds in pointy red hats calling themselves cardinals because Dad bought the job for them. Many priests can't read, absentee bishops take permanent vacations, and money is siphoned off to Rome, so popes can ride around with gold suits of armor, partying like they're Marc Antony in 44. B.C. No shaggy thong fun runs are conducted in public, but there's a whole lot of shaggy thonging going on behind closed doors.

And then, check this out: in April of 1517, Andreas Karlstadt goes to the Castle Church door and posts 151 theses. Yes, 151! That's a real value pack of theses. Folks, this is a full six months before Luther throws up his paltry 95 on the same door!

Watch Karlstadt stride up to the big doors with a hammer. Bang-bang-bang goes the hammer, up-up-up go the grievances. Does he take a moment to appreciate how they hang on the church door? Does he imagine that a crowd has formed behind him, desperate to push past him to take in the splendors of his critique? Does he await his elevation to a world-historical figure?

Well, whatever he might have imagined, nothing happens. No cheering crowds form around him. No printing presses spring to life. No one in Rome even hears a peep of it. One imagines Karlstadt taking a long, lonely walk back to his office to contemplate his continued obscurity. Perhaps he looks out the window as his 151 theses ripple in the wind on the door – no one there to read them – and shrugs, mumbling feebly, "It's the people's work..."

YOU'LL NEVER BELIEVE what happens next.

A former student, this punk kid Martin Luther (though, he is actually a few years older than Karlstadt) follows in his footsteps six months later, tacking 95 theses up on the same door, like a copycat who couldn't be bothered to come up with an extra 56 theses. But somehow, for some reason, Luther breaks into the big time. And I mean big time! Overnight! Printing presses thump day and night. Luther-mania tears across Europe. Poor Karlstadt. It can't be easy to have done something first in obscurity that is then copied to such great effect. Karlstadt's run at the door with a hammer and a nail gets him crickets, while Luther's prompts thunder, both applause from Germans and scorn from Rome.

This is the kind of turn of events that might lead to anger

issues in a person. It might see you massacring people in the name of salvation, or even yelling, "The people's work!" a bunch of times in front of a confused crowd.

Whatever the case, Luther soars while Karlstadt can only follow in his wake. Perhaps, as in comedy, all history is timing.

To his credit, Luther is a quick and funny guy. Once he grabs the spotlight, he holds it. After releasing his 95 theses, with its catchy hooks and familiar refrains, he remixes Matthew 16:18. It's a biblical passage that weighs in at 141 characters, little more than a haiku, but he manages to challenge the entire hierarchy of the Church in the process.

Genius!

It is at this time that Brother Martin Luther – priest, theologian, author, hymn writer, professor, Augustinian friar, and hipster – goes from being a voice in the crowd to setting his course on becoming "The Luther." It is at this moment that we imagine future screenwriters teaming up with future producers to begin shopping around for future leading men, directors, and yes, a large supporting cast: *Anyone know if we can find someone cheap to play this guy Karlstadt?*

But it didn't have to turn out this way. There is nothing inevitable about "The Luther" in 1517, 1521, or even 1530. Hindsight creates that illusion as if Luther were the product of an immaculate conception. With all the bright minds in Wittenberg, it could have easily been any one of the others who broke big time: "The Melanchthon," "The Müntzer," or even Karlstadt. He could have gone from being Andreas Karlstadt to becoming "The Karlstadt." Just imagine it. We would teach 151 theses in history class. Andreas Karlstadt King Jr. would give his, "I Have a Dream" speech. In this universe, Martin Luther would end up being the angry footnote, the fool in the crowd, the comic relief for the melodramatic biopic about Karlstadt.

And here's the thing, folks: this alternate reality almost happens. Because, in a twist right out of a Hollywood movie, something happens to Luther in 1521, and most people think he's dead.

And that, my friends, brings us to an apple cart, a dirt road, a dark night, and a burlap sack.

In 1521, Luther is summoned to the city of Worms for a meeting, also called a Diet. It's actually more of a trial, and Luther is being charged with heresy for his writings. And while I just said it is more of a trial, it's not actually going to be much of one. Clearly, Luther's writings are heretical, and Catholic Church leaders are demanding he recant. If he does, they'll be cool about the whole affair and let him live. Naturally, as Luther likes living but hates take-backs, he doesn't want to go to Worms at all. But it becomes increasingly unavoidable. The good news is there's a powerful guy looking after his interests: Frederick the Wise.

Now, let's take a minute to discuss Prince Frederick the Wise, Elector of Saxony, Landgrave of Thuringia. Frederick is Luther's patron at the University of Wittenberg and his protector out in the big, bad world. Can you guess why they call him Frederick the *Wise*? It's because he is *wise*. It is Frederick who keeps Luther alive, and it is Frederick who allows for the Reformation to proceed, thus establishing a level of independence from Rome for his people, his fiefdom. It's possible that the most important person in this chapter is not actually Luther but Fredrick. Because without Frederick the Wise, it's hard to imagine Martin Luther would have been anything but an ink stain on history.

"An ink stain on history." Has a nice ring to it, does it not? It's the kind of angry poetry I might find left behind on a student's desk. It is also the premise of my "Luther Fallacy," a little ditty of a thesis I've been workshopping over the years. While lecturing, I might say, "This is a good example of the Luther Fallacy." I'll pause, scan the room for derision, detect none, and proceed. Because they're teenagers, not yet able to sniff out academic pomposity. No one rolls their eyes. They wait expectantly for me to explain it or stare blankly at me or lay their head on their desk for a quick nap or check their phones.

But *you* want to know what the Luther fallacy is, right?

THE LUTHER FALLACY: A term created by noted author, historian, and educator Norm Coady in the early 21st century for the argument that social, political, and economic conditions are vastly more consequential than any action that can be taken by sole individuals. Mostly used to impress unsuspecting teenage students. This is the argument that Martin Luther does not actually matter that much in the grand scheme of things. His walk to a door in Wittenberg and his nailing of his 95 theses simply present the opportunity for larger and more powerful forces to leverage the moment, which has been centuries in the making.

In this reading of events, Luther is the religious and ideological cover for political and economic forces to proceed, particularly his patron Frederick the Wise but more generally a cadre of German Princes looking for independence from Rome. Seen this way, the Reformation is actually a regional war between the Mediterranean south and the Germanic north, a continuation of Rome's struggle with misbehaving barbarians. The fallacy here is thinking that Luther's walk to a Wittenberg church door changes history. It does not. It just fuels it. Or, put more simply, no single person is that important to the course of history. It is conditions that dictate events. To believe otherwise is to perpetuate a misunderstanding.

AND SO THERE YOU have it, my attempt at getting an entry in the *Stanford Encyclopedia of Philosophy*. While I won't hold my breath, I do stand by my convictions (*I can do no other*). And, paradoxically, while I scorn Great Man history, I so greatly admire Freddy the Wise that I will even toss him this superlative: Frederick the Wise is one of history's greatest patrons. It's true that Medici gets a lot of credit for funding great paintings and sculptures, and we all love standing in long, hot lines to spend five seconds looking at naked men with big heads. But Fredrick actually makes a world-historical transition possible.

For one, he keeps Luther alive, forcing Charles the V, Holy Roman Emperor, to pledge Luther's safe passage to and from the Diet of Worms. Luther can stand trial and even be convicted, but he must be returned to Wittenberg safely. So, even if found guilty, Luther can stay out of reach of the Church.

And so, Luther stands trial at Worms. He is asked to recant his works, and after a day or so of dithering, he refuses, saying, "My conscience is captive to the Word of God. Thus, I cannot and will not recant because acting against one's conscience is neither safe nor sound. Here I stand; I can do no other. God help me." This famous quote seems brave; though, it's actually a bit of a cop-out, and it does not satisfy his most ardent supporters. But it persists because it is beautiful and gracefully articulates the bind in which Luther finds himself: imminent death on one side, eternal damnation on the other. It is also a statement that leads to his conviction as a heretic, though the consequences are not clear, and the arrest won't come. Frederick the Wise has made sure of that, and Charles V has complied. Consequently, Luther is sent back to Wittenberg with an escort to assure him of a safe passage.

But on the journey, something really incredible happens, something right out of a big-budget Hollywood movie. It's almost more improbable than Luther waving a torch on the church steps. It's something that if you were watching for the first time, you might say, "No way did that happen."

But here's the thing, folks: It did.

IN THE MOVIE *LUTHER*, Luther and a monk buddy are being given "safe" conduct from Worms to Wittenberg. In Worms, there are plenty of powerful Catholics upset about Luther's existence, including Charles V. So, while we know Luther is supposed to be safe, the potential for a double cross is obvious. It's daytime, and the cart is on a dirt road when the guards suddenly peel off into the forest, abandoning Luther and his monk friend. In the next shot, it is night. Judging by the camera angle, something bad is about to happen. The cart driver suddenly stops, heading into the forest. Then, soldiers with torches emerge from the dark, rushing the cart, crossbows aimed at Luther's chest. The attackers approach and throw a burlap sack over Luther's head. In the next cut, we see Luther led into a room in a drafty castle, the camera slowly approaching as he is hunched over, the half-human. At last, the sack is removed. It takes a moment for his eyes to regain their focus. Ours, too. But when they do, they land on the friendly face of Spalatin, Frederick's secretary and staunch Luther ally.

Luther's relief is our relief. The burlap sack has not led to a shallow grave or a cold-water plunge but to the reversal we seek. Luther is safe in a fortress, and the movie can catch its breath. As can we.

Now, if you're waiting for me to tell you that this didn't happen, and this is the invention of a coked-up screenwriter, you're going to be waiting for a long time because it did happen – *kind of*. There's one major difference here, which is that Luther *knew* he was going to be kidnapped on the way back to Wittenberg and that it would be done by Frederick's men. The whole thing was pre-arranged.

Frederick's no dummy. He has no intention of letting Luther struggle to survive Rome's wrath out in the open. At the same time, he does not quite have the power to openly challenge Rome. And so, this fake kidnapping, and the subsequent cloistering of Brother Martin, who is renamed Knight George, gives Frederick the cover he needs, and the breath and beating heart that is so useful for Luther.

And now Luther is safely in the Wartburg Castle, and for the first time in a long time, able to dedicate himself to scholarly works in peace. He's finally gotten that sabbatical. He sets about translating the New Testament into German. Frederick has saved his monk from incurring the wrath of Rome, and Charles V has, in some ways, dodged a bullet. The danger has passed.

What could possibly go wrong?

Karlstadt. Andreas Rudolph Bodenstein von *Karlstadt*. That's what could go wrong, at least for Frederick. Because, with Luther hidden away in a Castle, a power vacuum opens. It's not like the Reformation is going to suddenly stop just so Luther can take a break in safety and crank out some translations. Luther started something big, and his absence isn't going to stop it. And as radical as Luther may appear to the eyes of Rome, back on the muddy streets of Wittenberg, there's a whole pack of theologians willing to take it further.

Like Karlstadt. He sees his chance to have his day in the sun, and he runs for it with open arms. He takes a posting in the small village of Orlamünde, which makes little Wittenberg look like a teeming Rome in comparison, and goes totally radical. He renounces all academic titles. He preaches against images in the Church or crucifixes around necks. For Karstadt, these are baubles disrupting true worship. He does the Eucharist without his vestments on and insists on being called "Brother Andreas." He makes Luther, who is off the scene, look like a conservative cardinal. Oh, and he marries a teenager, so there's that.

Karlstadt is basically unchained. Or unhinged. But he's having the time of his life. He got no airplay for his 151 theses, but now he's getting a cult following for his radical lyrics. He becomes what some people call, "The People's Prophet." He doesn't have Luther's scholarly chops, and he can't orate nearly as well, but he is more than willing to go blue and incite violence. His following grows. Statuary begins getting defenestrated, priests get harassed, and the powers in charge grow more and more nervous.

The problem is that Karlstadt represents not just a challenge against Rome but also to Frederick the Wise. He is going off the rails, attempting to remove the Church rather than reform it, and this is too far for Frederick. Even if Frederick were sympathetic theologically, which he is not, he does not have the political capital to cover such a move, and he knows it. He might be able to fake Luther's kidnapping, but Karlstadt is crossing a line. So, he does something wise and brings Luther out of the dugout, essentially instructing him, "Look, things are getting out of hand here, get out of Wartburg, come back, and cool things off."

Luther returns to Wittenberg and gives his famous 8 Sermons. He tells people that they need to *chill out*, that he is seeking the reform of the Church, not the elimination of it, insinuating that some people – *and I'm not mentioning any names here* – have gotten out of control and led people astray. Of course, everyone knows he is talking about Karlstadt.

He gives his argument theological justification, citing Jesus, who said, "Render therefore unto Caesar the things which are Caesar's and unto God the things that are God's." Put another way: worship the Lord and stay out of politics. For Luther, this is a conservative pivot, and it's hard not to see it as Luther doing Frederick's dirty work. But he owes his life to Frederick, and now he is returning that favor by coming back and canceling his old mentor, Karlstadt. We see Luther, in addition to being a scholar and leader, becoming a politician as well.

But we still have not located our climax scene with Karlstadt tossing priests downstairs and Luther charging in on a horse. Eight sermons filled with reproaches and passive-aggressive insinuations is a far cry from Luther screaming at Karlstadt, "Get out of Wittenberg before I beat you out!" followed by Karlstadt yelling, "It's the people's work!" and shoving a random guy before vanishing into history.

Where is our torch?

LIKE ANY ROCK star attempting a comeback, Luther takes his show on the road. It is, in fact, a regular Chill The "F" Out World Tour – or, at least, a tight circuit of central German hamlets where Luther can sermonize on the failing of radicals like Karlstadt and help boss Freddy to tap down the sparks of discontent.

He rolls into Jena, and unbeknownst to him, he has a special parishioner sitting in the back of the church, hiding under a felt hat. Guess who? That's right, Andreas Karlstadt has snuck into the crowd in Jena to hear Luther speak. He's heard rumors that his old pal is running him down, and now, he's come to hear the gospel of gossip for himself. Jena is close to Karlstadt's own tiny bastion of Orlamünde, and so theologically speaking, Luther is closing in on enemy territory. Karlstadt has come to head him off at the pass.

In a scene right out of a movie, Karlstadt hides in the back, scrutinizing Luther's words for condemnation. Obviously, it does not take long for Karlstadt to find offense. He must be positively smoldering with resentment in that pew, his mind drifting back to 1517 when he posted his 151 theses, and no one even bothered to read them. For years, Luther has outstripped him in every way. Now here Luther is, muscling into Karlstadt's humble dominion and bad-mouthing him, which is one of Luther's nasty habits. Even worse, the witty and sharp Luther is good at it and seems to be happy to take the robe off Karlstadt's back.

Karlstadt responds by sending a note to Luther, requesting a meeting.

They meet at a place called the Black Bear Inn, or Schwarzer Bär, which is still in operation and appears to be a depressingly efficient and clean place to spend a soulless night. There are portraits of Luther in the dining room and even a special Luther menu. I'm not sure how their appetizer of ox broth with egg custard and pepper dumplings relates to theological issues, but it sounds authentic (and by authentic, I mean hard to stomach; I think I'll pass).

But let's watch Luther and Karlstadt as they sit down for their little talk. There's no torch in sight, but there is probably a candle burning on the table as they engage in a depressingly passive-aggressive conversation.

Karlstadt accuses Luther of denouncing him as a murderous radical, and Luther smugly dodges the accusations by essentially saying, "Oh, really? Did I?" Karlstadt has a brief hissy fit or two during the conversation, the sad attempts of a wronged inferior. There is a bit of action when Luther abruptly stands up and tosses Karlstadt a coin. It is meant as a challenge, an open declaration that he is at odds with Karlstadt, and perhaps an invitation to an open debate.

But that is all it is. They probably finish their ox broth and egg custard and call it a night.

From there, Luther marches on, moving on to preach in Orlamünde, Karlstadt's postage-stamp-sized capital. It's not enough that Luther is the crown prince of the Reformation everywhere else; he must come to Karlstadt's bastion to stamp out his old mentor's fire.

But for once, "The Luther" does not carry the day. Because in Orlamünde Luther actually encounters a hostile crowd, faithful to Karlstadt. In fact, unlike the movie, it is Luther who is driven out of town, not Karlstadt. He is not even allowed to speak, and when he exits, church bells ring and a hyped-up Karlstadt declares, 'We who have heard the living voice of God beside the river Saale do not need to be taught by any monkish scribe!"

Karlstadt's glory is fleeting of course. Luther is firmly back on the Reformation scene now as his rock star self, sucking up all the oxygen, taunting Rome, and keeping Boss Freddy happy. Karlstadt never gets sufficient runway to truly lift off — to become "The Karlstadt." If Luther had stayed in Wartburg for a few more months, Karlstadtmania might have taken hold. True, Andreas is not half the speaker or writer as Martin, but his message is exceedingly appealing to the downtrodden. He is a real radical and has an agenda that truthfully bears more resemblance to Jesus's teachings than the shrewd and durable reforms of Martin Luther.

In any case, we may have found our torch at last; though, it might resemble a stick of vanilla-flavored incense more.

Taken together – the sermon in Jena, the spat at the Schwarzer Bär, and the rough welcome and exit Luther gets at Orlamünde – is just about as close to the torch scene in the movie as we are going to get. Indeed, it is far less dramatic, but it does have the requisite parts: Luther's disapproval of Karlstadt – Karlstadt's feeble response – and Karlstadt's angry supporters. In a sense, it even has Karlstadt's awkward "People's work!" exit from the scene, as Karlstadt is soon exiled by the authorities after Luther swings through town. He is never able to regain his balance again.

Now, if I were a screenwriter faced with this sequence of events – a boring sermon by Luther in Jena (though, I do like the cinematic twist of Karlstadt hiding under a felt hat in the back), a tepid back and forth between middle-aged men in a wayside inn, a non-event in Orlamünde – a sequence which would drag on the plot and likely suck up 30 minutes of the movie – I would be wise to condense it all into a two-and-a-half minute action-packed scene that includes a cool as hell dismounting, the torch routine, the flailing and hilariously campy Karlstadt, and a hot, smoldering Luther.

Moreover, this brief and fun scene, like much of the rest of the movie, demonstrates how much Luther is shaped by the people around him. Frederick forces Luther to become more political, which is wise if the revolutionary has hopes of surviving, and Luther does. He lives to an old age, married with children, presiding over a growing church. Karlstadt's antics and radical turn pop Luther out of Wartburg and put him back in the action, forcing him to moderate the ideas of the Reformation, which again contributed to the movement's long-term survival.

Seen this way, Luther is more like a balloon being batted back and forth. Because when Luther breaks away from the pack with his 95 theses, he becomes the property of many. That is part of being "The Luther" as opposed to Martin Luther. He is no longer a person. He is a phenomenon, and no one controls a phenomenon, not even the phenomenon themselves. And having said that, I must admit a funny thing just happened; I've changed my mind.

Am I allowed to do that? You might imagine that authors work everything out in advance when they write a book. Alas, no, not in my case. This is clearly an improvisational affair, like a classroom filled with teenagers.

In the process of researching and writing this chapter, I've reconsidered Luther's role in history. You might be pleased to hear that I am now ready to recant my *Luther Fallacy*. Thanks to the movie, and a bit of research, I've begun to see Wittenberg as an organic whole. If this chapter has taught me anything, it's that Luther wasn't so much a person as a coalition of people. "The Luther" isn't just Martin Luther; it's Martin Luther plus Frederick, Melanchthon, Müntzer, Karlstadt, and Fredrick's secretary Spalatin, along with many more.

The good news is that my reversal gives me another

candidate for the *Stanford Encyclopedia for Philosophy*, effectively doubling my chances.

THE WITTENBERG CONVERGENCE: A term created by noted author, historian, and educator Norm Coady in the early 21st century to refute the *LUTHER FALLACY*, also by Norm Coady, noted author, historian, and educator. This argument asserts that special factors were in place in Wittenberg that made it an ideal place from which to stage a protest against the Church in Rome. It benefited from its remote location, allowing theologians at the University of Wittenberg to share ideas in an environment unalloyed by ambition or papal reach. It also had uniquely qualified actors to play their roles, most notably Martin Luther, a shrewd monk and free thinker, and Frederick the Wise, a savvy prince and cautious politician. While Luther took the lead, Wittenberg was the beneficiary of many other thinkers who helped direct and redirect Luther to keep his message universal. Simultaneously, Frederick forced Luther to keep his message politically viable. Ultimately, Wittenberg serves as an example of how conditions, the course of events, and forceful and resourceful personalities can come together to change the world.

IN THIS CHAPTER, we have speculated whether Karlstadt could have been the star of the Reformation instead of Luther. But it probably doesn't matter. In the end, who cares who triggered the change? I doubt many people are rocking Martin Luther tattoos out there or that royalties are still rolling in for the 95 theses. (Although, I guess that Lutheran is easier to say than Karlstadtian.)

A more interesting question is whether Luther could have existed without Karlstadt or the other theologians of Wittenberg. Of course, he needed Frederick, but it could just as easily be claimed that Luther would never have matured intellectually without the companionship of Karlstadt and others who set up in the nowhere of Wittenberg and brought out the best in one another.

Seen this way, Martin Luther is just the lead singer of a supergroup named *The Re/Formers*. Melanchthon is on drums, Müntzer is on heavily distorted guitars, and Karlstadt is on bass. Frederick the Wise is their manager and Spalatin books all the gigs. They bicker a lot and frequently pass around cases of the moodies. They all want to be front and center. But they make some pretty interesting music together. And if that's the case, Karlstadt was right all along. In the end, the Reformation really is, "The people's work!"

This is what the film *Luther* demonstrates so well. The filmmakers could have easily left Karlstadt out of the script, but they did not. And because of that choice, they have left us to wonder just who the hell he was. And we have been encouraged to find out, and we have, kind of.

The film also crammed a bunch of other characters into its precious two-hour runtime. It lingered for long scenes not just on Frederick the Wise but also on his secretary Spalatin, one of the unsung heroes of the Reformation. It took us on a wild boar hunt with Pope Leo X and let us witness the simpering infighting between Cardinals with pointy red hats.

And at the center of it all, delicate as a flower, is Luther. At any point, we can imagine him cracking and vanishing, but the storm of people will not allow it. It makes *The Wittenberg Convergence*, a concept by notable historian Norm Coady, come to life and defies the predictability of most biopics where the titular character improbably bends the world around them to their will.

Believe it or not, there's something even more amazing about this film, particularly astounding when you consider its content: teenagers love it. Even 20 years later, when no one knows the actors on the screen, teenagers love it. They love seeing Karlstadt freakout. They can relate. They love the 95 theses montage sequence. It gets their blood pumping. And, of course, they love the torch. We all love torches.

And now, speaking of torches and teenagers, let's return to where all this Luthermania began, on October 31 – *Halloween* – of 1517. The world is about to change. A monk and scholar walk to a church door and nails up his 95 theses.

It's Martin Luther – not Melanchthon or Müntzer or Karlstadt. He is a resident of Wittenberg, not Berlin or Leipzig or Rome. He is being protected by Frederick the Wise, not Charles V or Albert of Mainz or Pope Leo X. He has taken some of the most important steps in human history followed by the second most consequential piece of hammering. He is stepping out of the crowd, committing himself to fate, and flirting with the possibility of being burned at the stake. For his pains, history will return to him again and again and again.

Brother Martin has taken his first real steps away from being a face in the crowd, a monk cloistered in a monastery, a scholar trapped in his own imagination. Armed with a hammer and a nail, he is about to become, "The Luther."

God help him.

Any similarities between these graphic novel frames and the 2003 Major Motion Picture *Luther* are purely coincidental, though you do have to admire an author who takes his obsession this far. Don't you?

Do I really need to explain this? Enjoy the details!

4

WAMPUM
JULY 3, 1754

GEORGE WASHINGTON HAS PUT himself in a terrible spot. He is 22 years old, a newly appointed colonel, and busy erecting a fort in the middle of a meadow in what we now call Western Pennsylvania. He calls it Fort Necessity, which is a massive understatement, and it looks more like a dog park for Cerberus. Logs split in half are bound together like an oversized hedge of frayed toothpicks, erecting what is basically a fenced area of grass.

Despite these rustic qualities, Washington is pleased, naïvely figuring the brook running across the meadow will provide ample drinking water during a siege. Later, he will have time to rethink this stroke of genius when there's a downpour in the middle of a battle and his so-called water supply turns his so-called fort into an actual swamp, dampening his cartridges and leaving him defenseless.

He is already six or seven major mistakes deep into a situation that is growing worse by the minute. In the last couple of weeks, he has erroneously attacked a French diplomatic mission and then botched the handling of his prisoners – and by "botched" I mean "allowed one of them to be slaughtered" – which will lead to an international incident, which will lead to a global conflict. He has followed these missteps with a campaign of covering his own ass that surely tests the claim that Washington, "Could not tell a lie." Because, in this case, even when not outright lying, he was aggressively mangling the truth. He has also overworked his men in a vain attempt to build a road to take on the French Fort Duquesne, badly underestimated the time it would take for reinforcements from Virginia to arrive, and failed to bring a rowdy bunch of South Carolinian regulars assigned to him under control. Seen this way, his pathetic fort feels more like an excuse to distract him from his problems, a piece of busy work before the apocalypse. Indeed, with 1,600 French and Indian troops marching his way, Washington is facing steep odds. Or even imminent death.

Nearby, very much disapproving of the entire scene, is the Native American leader Tanghaisson, better known as "the Half King." Washington would not be in this mess were it not for him, but that is not going to keep the sage semi-chief from shooting baleful looks at young Washington and muttering to his own people about the futility of the endeavor. Indeed, he seems to relish Washington's every misstep in that special way older men cultivate when under the command of much younger men. Wherever Washington turns, whatever task he undertakes, the Half King is lurking nearby, sniffing dismissively.

But he's not exactly wrong, either. The water crossing Fort Necessity is not even the biggest issue. Far more concerning is the fact that Washington has elected to place his fort in the middle of a meadow on fairly low land surrounded by nearby forest. Take a moment and picture this in your mind: a lonely fort in the middle of a ring of nearby trees that will allow the French to take up fortified positions and fire at will. Thought of another way, Washington's fort is more like target practice, leaving the real fortress of the forest to the French. So, if you're the Half King and have pointed this out, only to have this young man natter on about abundant water supply...well, perhaps you have the right to be a bit annoyed.

Politically, Washington isn't doing himself any favors either. He does give the Half King and his men wampum, which is a well-received recognition of their service, but he squanders that goodwill shortly thereafter by referring to a much younger Native American as first in council. He also treats the Half King and his men as if they are under his command, which they are not, ordering them to dig trenches before his pathetic excuse for a fort or sending them out on scouting missions.

The latter confirms the obvious: the French have vastly larger and better-supplied forces that are rapidly closing in on Washington's meadow fort. And this is probably why the Half King and his group quietly slip into the forest and disappear. They may be pro-British, they may despise the French, but they are not fools. They much prefer to live.

Now Washington and his exhausted men are trapped in their fort of necessity and can hear the French coming. They are sitting ducks. Coincidentally, it begins to rain. Hard. Incessant sheets of rain. Washington's cherished water supply spreads out into large puddles soaking their feet. Gunfire grows louder and sharper. Then, the sizable French force appears at the forest edge.

Perhaps this is the moment that Washington thinks to himself that the Half King was right. This is certain death. Some of his men, feeling the same, break into the rum supply and commence to get drunk. With the mud, the endless sheets of rain, and the drunkenness, it all has the feeling of a music festival gone wrong with the added risk of being shot by musket balls.

And it is at this moment that Washington must know his future is very much in doubt. Worse, he is so very far away from home. If these are his final moments, little will be known about them. He will be finished before he even begins. What a shame: Just 22 years old and George Washington is preparing for a pointless, nameless death in the middle of nowhere.

IT REALLY IS the middle of nowhere unless you're a mosquito. Yes, there are the Ohio River Valley Indians, but they have a limited voice in their own affairs and must suffer the indignity of Iroquois proxies like the Half King controlling their region.

It is actually this nowhereness that makes this place attractive because it is very much up for grabs. A small group of rapacious British and French colonists, along with representatives of the Iroquois, have become interested in the convergence of two rivers in a place we now call Pittsburgh.

Never mind that empire heavies in faraway London, Paris, or Onondaga know next to nothing about this land. They cannot knowledgeably discuss the convergence of the Ohio and Allegheny Rivers or explain its potential. They will glaze over if you try to engage them in conversation about beaver pelts and trading posts, and worse, they may begin to wonder why so much money is being wasted to secure obscure parts of the world that can never really pay off. Even most colonial leaders in Montreal and Williamsburg are not interested in this piece of nowhere. Truth be told, we can count the main players on two hands, and their resources are scant.

But the struggle is real, and the issue is one of trade, chiefly in beaver pelts. It is easy to forget that much of North American exploration and early infrastructure focused entirely on covering the heads of Europeans with beaver pelt hats. Not coon skin caps, the ones with the tails hanging out the back, but beaver pelts, wonderfully malleable into any shape and brilliantly water resistant. Brutal wars are fought to control its trade with the British, French, and Dutch vying for the most pelts at the cheapest price. This, in turn, supplies the Iroquois Confederacy and the Hurons with the weapons to wage their own wars of inland supremacy.

It is, in short, an epic bloodbath. The survivors send a steady supply of pelts off to the hatteries in Europe where workers use mercury to separate the long fur of the beaver from the pelts and go as "Mad as a Hatter!"

Behold, my friends, history at its most depressing: a beaver apocalypse, the genocide of the Huron, and the slow poisoning of people looking to do an honest day's work – all for stupid-looking hats whose fashions change mostly to keep the hat shops in business. Sound familiar?

The beaver arena becomes an extension of long-standing British-French tensions with Native American tribes perfectly ready to play these strange and highly paranoid groups off one another. By and large, the French have better relations with the Native Americans. This is partly because the French do not so much establish colonies as they do forts — trading posts filled with finished goods to give as gifts — and keep up good relations and hopefully not get killed – as it turns out, an expensive way to pay the rent. Or, put another way, the French play nice because they have no other alternative. Whereas the British, with their superior numbers, play rough – pushing tribes westward and conducting small-scale slaughters when it feels proper and necessary to do so.

But as mean as the British can be, they have one thing going for them: better stuff at cheaper prices. Their industrial revolution is gathering steam, while the French are still concerned with the hemlines of fancy dresses and cheese production. British factories pump out goods at an increasingly alarming rate with better designs done cheaper.

What this mostly amounts to, at least in our conversation, are better guns. For the tribes, this is more important than just trying to figure out the perfect dishwasher for your new kitchen. This is a question of life and death. If you're exhausting your beaver supply through overzealous trapping, you will need to expand your operation, and that task is made vastly simpler when you have a military advantage. Conversely, your neighboring tribes might be exhausting *their* beaver supply. They, too, might get it in their mind to seek expansion, shopping for the best weapons at the lowest price.

Consequently, more and more tribes begin to ghost French trading posts in favor of the British. All the diplomatic goodwill slowly built up by the French over a century evaporated, leaving them with few options outside of coerced trade and armed conflict. For the French, the once-lucrative venture of Canada is becoming a sad, cold disappointment. Much time has been spent humoring chiefs in ceremonies that stretch on for days. Goods have been gifted to keep the prospect of trade alive. And then there's that magical, uniquely regional treasure whose value goes far beyond any mere coin or note.

Wampum.

Lots and lots and lots of wampum.

. . .

YES, wampum, small cylinders produced from shells that can be placed along a string, making decorative belts. While in the simplest sense, these beads can be seen as a form of currency among the Indians and the colonists, in reality, they were both more and less important than money. In fact, after the arrival of the Europeans, and the subsequent inflation of the beads, the main use of wampum was not to purchase goods, which would more likely be done directly in beaver pelts and other goods. Instead, they served as the diplomatic glue of the continent, cementing intentions, creating peace, or even declaring war. To accept wampum was to bind yourself to a people or a cause, and so wampum established relations between tribes and with the colonists.

This understanding of wampum brings me back to 5th grade when the fad was placing tiny beads on safety pins, which were then given out as tokens of friendship. Chiefly, this was a pastime of the girls, but I became so enamored by the display that I convinced my mother to set me up with a small factory, which I used to produce a large number of friendship beads for myself (circumventing the need to network for them).

And that's how, one morning, I showed up at the Franklin School and entered Ms. Gladwin's class wearing so many friendship beads on my collared t-shirt that I looked like a little tin pot dictator. Mussolini would have envied me.

But I'd overdone it. Classmates began to inquire about the origin of my honors, protective of the value of this new currency. No number of vague answers or allusions to friends in neighboring towns satisfied their suspicions. Slowly, discreetly, my friendship safety pins were removed and placed out of sight, many ending up in the trash can, my shirt now a mess of pin sized holes. Clearly, I would not have lasted long in the 18th Century Ohio River Valley.

Wampum might also be compared to Bitcoin as its value came from the labor that went into its production instead of the rarity of its material. Typically, a person working all day with a flint could produce maybe 20 to 25 beads, a fraction of the total needed for a single belt. Add to that labor the inland demand for the beads, the associated transportation costs, which come at a premium due to its value, and a belt with hundreds of beads becomes an object of real value.

And where there is wealth, there is danger. For the coastal Algonquin, so near shells and so skilled at creating the beads, wampum was a blessing...until it was not. They were conquered by others desirous of their bead factories – first by the Iroquois then the British and French.

And, of course, where there is value, there is scarcity. At times, wampum paucity became so acute that the French took apart and reworked belts in their possession, so they could regift them. They tried to introduce glass beads mass-produced in Europe as an alternative, and when this failed, they even introduced Cowrie snails into the New World, so they could farm their shells. My god, what could possibly be more French than trying to fix an issue of consumption by introducing snails into the situation?

As we've seen, the French are highly reliant on this gift

economy, and as a result, wampum is far more important for them than money, particularly inland, in the honor-driven world of the Native Americans. Lacking the apparatus for occupation or the desire to hold land the way Europeans are accustomed to, tribes gain their value and standing through their word.

What wampum represents, sometimes beautifully and sometimes cynically, is a spoken shared purpose made concrete. In fact, this is what they are called: speech belts. Perhaps this is why Louis XV ordered four million beads in anticipation of the goodwill needed to sustain the French in the Americas during the Seven Years' War. That represented a whole lot of sweet talk, goodwill being converted from livres into beads to be blanketed over a continent to support colonial Gallic ambitions.

Alas, that much sweet talk can easily fade into sweet nothings. Or, put another way, the more wampum flying around, the less it's worth. Any cunning chief worth their salt might see the writing on the wall and embrace a more transactional view of affairs. Do I want a pretty speech belt, or do I want guns with which I can blow away the heads of my competition? Perhaps, as did my classmates, the Indians begin to question the origin of these beads and wonder at the stability of the entire system. The tribes and the beaver pelts may begin to further drift from the French, who could be left with so many musket ball sized holes in their shirts.

. . .

TANGHAISSON, for one, is tiring of wampum. He is cunning, he is transactional, and he has been drifting away from the French for some time. He is known to us as *the* Half King, but he's actually one of several half kings in the region. When referring to him specifically in this book, we will capitalize the term Half King. And while this English and French honorific might seem more like a diminishment, it's actually an attempt to classify a complex role.

As a half king, Tanghaisson functions as a proxy for the mighty Iroquois of the north, overseeing vassal tribes in the Ohio Valley, the Shawnee, and the Delaware, as well as the Mingo people, who were expatriated Iroquois, akin to British colonists in Virginia. In fact, you might think of Tanghaisson as a colonial governor of a kind, but the analogy isn't exact. Tribal power structures are fluid, less hierarchical, and more improvisational.

Half kings like Tanghaisson are not allowed to speak for the Iroquois council, nor do they have the apparatus of a colonial venture – no armies, no sitting government, scant resources. Seen this way, they are more like ¼ kings, something between a fixer and a babysitter. But this is not quite right either because the French and English, loathed to deal with the Iroquois directly, encouraged the half kings to expand their powers. So, in this way, they might be ⅘ kings; though, they often had difficulty wrangling the Indians under their "control" to do anything, so let's level that out to ¾ kings.

Tanghaisson is nothing if not ambitious. He is fluent in

many languages, and whatever's there to see, he's seen it. He is now in the Ohio Valley, overseeing the Delaware and the Shawnee for the Iroquois, and in possession of some nice French wampum, but he does not prefer the French. Not at all, in fact. He wants an alliance with the British. And why does he prefer the British? Well, for one, maybe the French boiled and ate his father, perhaps with a side of Cowrie snails in a rich butter and garlic sauce. So obviously, that's bad. But the more pressing issue is that the French are likely to stir up the Shawnee and Delaware to overthrow their Iroquois masters, and that includes Tanghaisson himself.

He has good cause to be worried. The French are descending from the north like spiders on threads of their own making, a reaction to their dwindling trade prospects, attempting to block British advancement westward by any means necessary. French delegations glide down rivers in big canoes dressed in full military regalia, halting periodically to nail French royal coats of arms to trees and bury lead plates in the ground with the date upon them.

This ritual is customary European protocol for property markings, and even today, in the Commonwealth of Massachusetts, I can go to the edge of my property to find lead cylinders buried in the soil. For the Indians, this ritual is a curiosity, a somewhat absurd performance, until they figure out the true meaning of it all. Annoyed, they wait for the French to leave, tear down the royal coats of arms off the trees, and dig up the lead plates, melting them down for their own purposes or sometimes handing them over to the

English in a show of fidelity. But those very same Indians may then go back to the French and tell them that the English dug the plates up, attempting to sow discord. Because, in accordance with ancient wisdom, and probably the first lesson ever learned by man, working your opponents off one another is a pretty neat trick.

There is an Iroquois saying that you can't live in the woods and be neutral. And while this may be true, it doesn't mean your allegiances need to be set in stone. If anything, all sides in this affair have a tendency toward overcommitment, which is a nice way of saying duplicity. There is a certain promiscuity regarding alliances. Wampum belts fly off the rack, and declarations of eternal friendship mix freely with plenty of rum and wine. Friends, frenemies, friends of enemies, passing strangers, opportunistic acquaintances – the dense forest by the forks of the Ohio is filled with them, and they are all looking out for number one. Half king proxies quietly exceed their powers while corrupt French fort masters skim profits and British colonial governors send youngsters beyond borders into the wilderness against the interests of their own sovereign.

Folks, this is no mothballed lesson about a mini fight before the American Revolution; it is a savage reality show in the middle of nowhere. The fact is that no one has come to this forest to make friends – no matter how much wampum they toss around.

As a matter of fact, the Half King is presently conspiring to make one of those show-stopping moves where tense music is introduced, and a commercial break follows. He is about to return a speech belt to the French, a rejection of the relationship. Not only that but he is going to force the Shawnee and Delaware to do the same with their wampum. But he knows he can only get away with this if he has a safe place to land – an ally at the ready who can push back against the Cowrie-snail-loving, lead-plate-burying, pot-stirring French bastards.

Enter 21-year-old George Washington.

Were this, in fact, a reality show, this would provide a moment of comic relief – the affable, eager, and fresh-faced Washington presenting himself as the camera cuts to and lingers upon the highly chiseled visage of Tanghaisson: Half King not happy. Here, he is doing his best to hold the region and the British send a callow youngster and a few flunkies, a phenomenon of underwhelming British moves that will follow us for the rest of the chapter, culminating in a dangerously unimpressive fort in the middle of a wide-open meadow, surrounded by a dense forest, shortly due to become a flooded swamp surrounded by a dense forest.

THEY FIRST MEET in December of 1753. While the French are sending legions of soldiers to seize the forks of the Ohio, Washington arrives armed only with a diplomatic communique politely requesting that the French refrain from molesting British traders. The Half King, seeing this pitiful British response, does his best to beef up Washington's small delegation with Ohio warriors but can only muster a small handful from the tribes, who also refuse to return their wampum belts to the French. His worst fears are confirmed as he realizes that the tribes under his control have no intention of pivoting against the French. Why would they? The French are muscling into the region like a freight train while the British are dropping off sternly worded letters. So, at this point, Tanghaisson looks not like a king half full but a king half empty.

Tanghaisson, Washington, and their skeleton crew land at Logstown, a small fort where the French officers are so secure in their future dominance of the region that they wine and dine Washington's delegation and openly crow about their plans. Of course, there are ulterior motives to their hospitality, and both the Half King and Washington are keenly aware that the French are actively courting the Indians in their command, plying them with wampum and rum, enticing them to stay and forge friendships.

Neither Washington's letter nor Tanghaisson's return to the wampum belt can be handled in such a remote outpost as Logstown, so they are forced to proceed deeper into French territory to Fort Machault. Much the same scene unfolds there with the Half King and the Ohio Indians being wined and dined by French officers. Tanghaisson manages to return the speech belt but then succumbs to a charm offensive by the French. Along with rum and wampum, the French ply him with guns, and Washington can only watch the seduction unfold as the letter from Virginia wrinkles limply in his pocket.

Now, it is young Washington's turn to be exasperated, this time with a flattered old Half King caving to French flirtations. Washington wants to leave the fort, but the Half King resists, which is the geopolitical equivalent of having a romantic prospect refuse to leave a party you wish to exit. Washington feels like a heel. He makes his own way back to Virginia, an action-packed journey that includes being shot at, falling through the ice, and nearly freezing to death. Just think how differently American history would have turned out if Washington were just a little less lucky during this comedy of errors.

A few months later, the British build a rather lame fort at the forks of the Ohio and the Allegheny, hanging the front door just a day before the arrival of a large French force. They needn't have bothered though because the French pop that same door off the hinges without firing a shot.

The French, happy with their new digs, graciously give provisions to British soldiers for their trip back to Virginia and send them packing. Washington is not there, but the Half King is, and he can't believe what he's seeing. No shots fired?! Provisions for a trip home?! Peace?! Tanghaisson is disgusted and desperate. No one wants to be boiled alive and eaten, but this death by a thousand cuts isn't great, either. At every turn, the British underwhelm, and in each encounter at their side, the Half King loses face with the tribes that he is supposedly a fractional sovereign over.

The good news – *kind of* – is that George Washington is returning from Virginia with troops. In reality, these troops barely qualify as soldiers, and they've been sent to reinforce a fort that's technically no longer in their possession. Plus, as Tanghaisson knows, Washington is young and green. Very, very young and green.

But fundamentally, the Half King is a realist, and he works with what is given to him. Maybe young and green is just what he needs.

Washington is on his way.

ONE THING TANGHAISSON has going for him is clarity. He needs to get the British into a war with the French. Not a wine-laced discussion, not a skirmish, not a friendly surrendering of forts but a full-blown, no-turning-back war. The bigger the better. He also, as it turns out, realizes that he can benefit from Washington's youth. What might have posed a challenge at first will now be his best opportunity. He doesn't need Washington to be bold or savvy or even survive the trip. He just needs to get him into an epic piece of trouble, binding the British to his cause. Because no string of wampum is as good as a pile of scalps.

As it turns out, Washington is primed for manipulation, mostly because he is freaking out. He arrives too late to reinforce the fort at the forks and commences to build a road for further reinforcements coming to mount a counterattack, working his troops to the point of delirium. He is also intensely concerned about reports of French in the area. He finally finds a meadow to rest his troops – yes, *that* meadow, the *Great* Meadow, the one with the refreshing brook.

The Half King sends him messages that the French are closing in on him (they are not). Washington sends scouts out to confirm. They find nothing, but somehow this absence only creates more anxiety for Washington, as if no evidence only means the French are both numerous and sneaky.

He's paranoid enough to begin Fort Necessity, which should be called Fort Panic; though, he does call its location a "charming field for an encounter" as if the coming battle with the French were to be a sexual tryst. If nothing else, he is right: somebody is about to get (bleeped out).

Nearby, a small group of French troops move through the forest, led by a mid-level officer named Jumonville to…

Well, folks, here is where the debate will begin because the purpose of Jumonville's mission is a bit of a mystery. The British, specifically Washington, later contend that Jumonville's group represents a war party. All we know for sure is that he carries a letter stating that all British should immediately exit French lands. But, in addition to this message, spying could be part of his task as well and would be pretty much par for the course. It is less likely that they are a fighting force. They are too few in number to cause that kind of trouble.

When Washington and the Half King come upon Jumonville and his men, they are camped in a glen, possibly to hide their position (suggesting spycraft) but more likely to keep dry during the rain (implying diplomacy and common sense). No sentries are posted (again, diplomacy, but less common sense), and their guns are stacked together outside their tents (um... *diplomacy*), and everyone, except one soldier who is taking a leak, is asleep in their tents (DIPLOMACY!). If Washington were not so wound up, and the Half King so keen on winding him tighter, he might have considered all these factors.

He does not. He descends on Jumonville's encampment in the glen and makes quick work of it. Fifteen minutes later, Washington and the Half King's men are mopping up. Washington allows tomahawking of the wounded, a courtesy to tribe members fighting alongside him but spares those who remain intact. He formally takes the French officers prisoner, securing them their rights. As an officer, being captured is more like being taken out for a fancy meal with both British and French officers tripping over themselves to be hospitable to those who have obtained the same level of class and standing as themselves. Washington and Jumonville are playing the same game – the kind that allows forts to be transferred with no shots fired. The Half King is not.

Jumonville, probably a little shocked by the rude awakening, is actually injured and so technically eligible for tomahawking. But he feels secure in his new position as a captured officer, and he motions for the British to gather, so he can read the message he's been sent to convey.

It's a pathetic scene as the warning to stay off French land is obviously muted by his compromised circumstance. Washington, in another trend-setting-first for the American character, only speaks English, so he has no idea what is being read. Tanghaisson, on the other hand, is fluent in French, not to mention power dynamics, and knows where these words are heading. The letter is of a diplomatic nature – a spot of wampum, not musket fire – and will be proof that Washington has stumbled into a diplomatic incident, not a victory.

Perhaps wishing to keep things brief, or looking to censor words coming next, or maybe simply looking to make the coup complete, the Half King strides toward Jumonville, who is on the floor, raises his tomahawk, and says, "Tu n'es pas encore mort, mon père." ("You are not dead yet, my father.")

THEN, he strides forward and splits Jumonville's skull open with a tomahawk blow. From this newly open cavity, he scoops out some of Jumonville's warm brains and washes his hands with them. The same brain that, seconds before, heard the words signaling impending death is now dripping between the fingers of the Half King. Perhaps there are thoughts still racing through that cranial matter as it is spread on Tanghaisson's hands, the last surprised volts of electricity for a mid-level French officer dying in the middle of nowhere, just another extra in the big show of history.

It does not take more than a second for Washington, brains still securely in his own cranium, to weigh the gravity of this act. This is *bad*. *So* bad. Very, *very* bad. And let's take a moment and state the obvious just in case you find yourself in a soggy glen with a bunch of prisoners: you must never – *never ever* – execute a diplomat, as that person is vulnerable by design. Without vulnerable people, messages cannot be sent. Where diplomats cannot breathe, diplomacy cannot proceed. Even Washington, young and inexperienced as he is, knows this, probably even before the Half King goes to wash his hands in Jumonville's brains. This is a hot, hot mess.

The Half King makes it worse, stoking the hot coals to get his fire roaring. He sends a messenger to the French disclosing that Washington has allowed the slaughter of Jumonville, conveniently omitting his own prominent role as head splitter, and rather outrageously claiming he had done his best to keep the murder from happening. He then refuses to meet with British representatives to back up the young Washington and provide him with needed cover.

Meanwhile, Washington is now in possession of two highly credible French officers who will be sent to his sponsor, Dinwiddie. Inevitably, they will share with him what they saw, which is that Jumonville had been killed in cold blood. No amount of wampum will tidy up this disaster.

Washington goes into damage control, sending letters back to Dinwiddie making detailed points regarding the malicious intentions of Jumonville's spying party. They read very much like a young man who has majorly messed up protesting too much. He might be better served saying nothing or even confiding in Dinwiddie that, perhaps, certain mistakes had been made. But instead, the mythological Washington of cherry tree fame comes across as something even worse than a liar – a full-blown equivocator of the first order. He's a teenager who has wrecked the family car and is hiding it in the mistaken belief that everything will be okay if he can just find the right color of spray paint to cover the scratches. If nothing else, the good and bad news is that his reputation is the least of his problems.

He has barely erected his sad excuse for a fort when word comes that the French and Indians are closing in on their position. It is at this point that the Half King and his men exit, disappearing into the dustbin of history. He has successfully engineered a war between the British and the French but has no intention of sticking around to die in it. Now, Washington is left with his own pitiful excuse for a force, plus the regulars from South Carolina who refuse to lift a finger, content to let doom close in on them.

Then, it begins to rain. A real soaker. Of course, it does. And seeing as Washington is sitting in a sunken meadow with brooks running across it, everything starts getting wet: candles, matches, and cartridges, all those super useful items in times of darkness and war.

With no candles, it is kind of hard to keep control of your soldiers, and maybe that's why they break into the rum supply. But it doesn't matter because the cartridges are wet, and the guns won't work anyway. Meanwhile, the French and Indians are having a great time with their target practice on the pathetic fort, and it feels like only a matter of time before the French allow them all to be slaughtered in the same fashion that Jumonville was slaughtered.

And just when death seems certain, and Washington can only pray, he gets lucky. Exceedingly lucky. The French are having so much fun with their turkey shoot that they begin running out of ammo. For all they know, British reinforcements might soon arrive, and so the French, having already taken the fort at the forks, settle for a dominant victory instead of a wholesale slaughter of Washington's men. They offer terms of surrender for his inspection.

There's just one problem. As neither Washington nor his troops speak French, and the Half King has departed, they are forced to send a Dutchman, Van Braam, to receive the terms from the French. Unfortunately, Van Braam barely speaks French or English, and this is a bad combination because he only half understands what he must half explain. So, he's kind of a ¼ translator. This would have been less of a problem if the candles of Fort Necessity could be lit to view the papers. But they are wet like everything else.

Washington's ingeniously convenient water supply has left him flummoxed as to the terms of the capitulations. They grill the Dutchman for details but get very little from him. For want of a candle, or a polyglot Nederlander, Washington signs capitulations without knowing what they really say. And this is kind of important because one of the lines in the first paragraph states, "As our intention had never been to trouble the peace... but only to revenge the assassination which has been done on one of our officers, bearer of a summons..."

As blind as a bat but lacking the accompanying sonar or

even the instincts for what might be in the document and having totally put himself at the mercy of the French – and, of course, very much desiring to live – Washington signs the capitulations, unknowingly accepting the official designation of assassin.

This admission will become the cornerstone of the French case against the British as the incident spills out of the Ohio Valley and swamps the larger world over the next seven years. No amount of wampum can cleanse this blemish from Washington's record, and that stain spreads from the nowhere of Ohio to Quebec to Prague to Calcutta and so many other locations around the world where the British and French will knock heads. In many ways, this Seven Years' War is the world's first global war, and its roots are in a damp glen in the middle of nowhere where a hatchet is used on a wounded officer.

"You are not dead yet, my father."

It's such a great line. Shakespearean. We might spend a chapter trying to decode it. Is it literal? If so, it seems almost helpful, as if the Half King is simply trying to assist a wounded Jumonville to the other side. Is it meant as an allusion to the French status in the American interior, a way of pointing out their weakness and trying, to the best of his ability, to dispatch not just Jumonville but all the Gauls out of Ohio? Or, seeing as it is possible the French boiled and ate his father, is this the Half King's attempt to free his father's suspended spirit? This last explanation is highly unlikely, which is why I like it the best.

We will never know for sure. Wampum in hand, the Half King vanishes into a forest where no records are kept, no memoirs penned. He will shortly die of illness. Only Washington, and the clumsy Dutchman, remain alive to be blamed.

Washington, the youngster tricked into killing a diplomat. He has done nothing but blunder since entering the Ohio Valley and now will be forced home a failure. See him as he is, age 22, soaked to the bone in a muddy meadow not even able to light a candle, a bunch of drunk soldiers stumbling around him and not paying him a whit of attention.

Behold the father of our nation.

THIS IS, obviously, not the George Washington we're acquainted with. We're familiar with the Godlike portrait staring down at our first-grade desk or the superlative-laden biography lying on our bedside table. We know the timeline. It begins with a splintered cherry tree, a subsequent bout of irrepressible honesty, and ends with a farewell speech that ranks as one of the most consequential documents in American history. In between, there are just so many other accomplishments of a man who rightfully deserves the honorific of Founding Father. Even those gripped with dissenting revisionist fever know well enough to leave Washington alone, instead drawing their knives on Jefferson, and unbelievably, Lincoln. But Washington? He is Zeus-like – so consequential and powerful as to almost be faceless. Power undisputed, his gravitas intact, he strides across American history like a giant so large that no one dares make a closer inspection of him.

That version of Washington is legendary, a near Godhead to aspire to. A colossus.

And boring. Lifeless and dull. Impossible to teach.

What makes his status all the more interesting is the fundamental mediocrity of the man himself – he is not a particularly good speaker, writer, or military strategist. Outside of his height, he is seemingly bereft of natural gifts.

We have met Caesar in this book, blessed in almost every regard. But Washington, of the wide hips, the wooden teeth, and the muted voice, is not the stuff of empire pathfinder.

To his credit, he did not even want to be president and suffered through two terms only to wind up attacked and belittled by a pack of squabbling youngsters mucking the nation up – not even a half king, a husk of a president. One gets the sense that Washington grew to be like Tanghaisson, an older man who has seen it all and must put up with a bunch of delinquent know-it-alls with delusions of grandeur. One can easily imagine an older Washington reflecting on his younger self, the one so excited about having a water source during a siege, and just shaking his head at the futility of it all, maybe thinking, "The Half King really was right – I should have called it Fort Disaster."

While all of this might seem like a critique of our first president, it is not. It is the opposite. This understanding of Washington's inherent commonness makes him all the more unique in history. It's not his abilities that sing but his limitations. It is not his honesty, but his selectiveness when releasing information and how he spins it to cause the least harm – to himself and to his mission. Who wants a president who cannot tell a lie? He is not proactive; he is improvisational. And if we listen closely to his song, we might find a better way to understand – and teach – the man, his real genius, and his secret gift.

What we should be presenting in schools is Washington at age 22, not 44, 57, or 65. Let's study Washington getting conned into attacking a diplomatic mission, grossly botching the taking of prisoners, baldly obfuscating to cover his backside, and then proceeding to build a fort in the worst possible place. If we teach this version of Washington, and we already know the rough outline of the rest, it begs some useful questions: How did such a young fool become such an important man? What changed between the time he let his gunpowder get wet in a muddy field and the time he cornered the world's greatest power at Yorktown? What qualities lead to greatness in those of middling ability?

Twenty-four years after his surrender to the French, 250 miles east of Fort Necessity, Washington finds himself freezing with another group of underequipped malcontents at Valley Forge. He has just suffered a string of failures with defeats at Brandywine, Paoli, and Germantown as well as the loss of Philadelphia, the rebel capital, to the British.

He and his men must now survive the deprivation of a discontented winter – starvation and disease ripping through the encampment as the revolutionaries huddle against the cold, attempting to stay alive, both personally and as a fighting force. Two thousand men will die in this quiet battle. Meanwhile, Washington is unable to get the support he desperately needs, and his power is challenged on all sides. But he holds on. He holds on, tightens his grasp on power, and revitalizes his army. Because that is what Washington does. He holds on. He holds on despite the odds, and he does it quietly. So quietly and patiently does he hold on that his performance demands that those around him do the same. He endures in a way that brings endurance to others. This is the genius of a man who has slowly and painfully gathered his plain greatness.

He does not have many friends. His own men flirt with mutiny; some simply walk away. The Continental Congress has all but abandoned the cause, refusing further funding for the dying army. But he is not abandoned by his Indian allies, the Oneida. They bring corn into the camps of Valley Forge and need to physically restrain the soldiers from eating the corn raw, knowing it will swell their stomachs and kill them. Polly Cooper, an Oneida woman, remains to show the soldiers how to store and cook the corn. She is offered payment but refuses as she feels it is her moral duty to aid these men and payment would cheapen that value. In gratitude, the wives of the soldier and possibly even Martha Washington, though this is not verified, present Polly Cooper with a black shawl. It is a delicate piece – semi-transparent in parts like a veil – and it still exists, a part of Oneida's history. It is not wampum, but it is like wampum, an object of dedicated labor that is a means to forge an alliance and acknowledge a debt that goes deeper than coinage.

Spring comes, and with it, light.

On the 6 of May 1778, the cannons and muskets of Valley Force erupt repeatedly in response to a joyous piece of news that has just arrived in the camp. The French – yes, *the French* – have formally allied themselves with the rebels, a major coup for the colonist's cause.

What does Washington think of it all, to hear his soldier huzzah, "Long Live the King of France!" and to see them come to life again with love in their hearts for the Cowrie-snail-eating, lead-plate-burying French? He fought them near the forks and now they are his saviors; later, of course, he will discard them like a speech belt whose strings have snapped, scattering wampum into the mud underfoot. Like the Iroquois, he plays his enemies off one another to keep his own people free. It's a good trick if you can pull it off.

As Washington watches the musket fire and the cannons bellow, I like to imagine the giant ghost head of the Half King looking down from the Sky World. Yes, it's a little cheesy, I know, but we're talking about Washington here.

At long last, Tanghaisson gives George Washington a nod of approval, just a few centimeters of support up and down. It is begrudging, years in the making, and all the more powerful for its restraint. Tanghaisson might not have agreed with the particulars of the agreement, but he would have appreciated the play and how very far Washington has come since planting that ill-advised fort in a depressed meadow.

A comically incorrect and patently unfair French rendering of what happened with the Jumonville Party, which was bad enough that it need not be exaggerated. The white flag and clutched diplomatic papers are a nice touch, though.

Hey everybody! I found the perfect place for a fort. It's in a sunken meadow with streams nearby and it's also surrounded by forest which will provide our enemy the perfect protection why they take pot shots at us.
Hope it doesn't rain!

Let's be honest: More effort went into this diorama of Fort Necessity then went into the original building of Fort Necessity. The pooling meadow water in the background is a nice touch. That'd be an A+ in my gradebook!

A sadly accurate depiction of Washington and his men trying to get enough light to read the French terms for surrender. They never do get a candle lit, and Washington accepts French demands, sight unseen, tacitly admitting to murdering Jumonville in the process. Whoops!

5

PAPER CUP, PART 2
JANUARY 14, 2014

I AM on the top floor of the High School of Commerce in Springfield, Massachusetts, covered in coffee. The cup lies decapitated near the staircase, its top having skidded out across the hall, and the sleeve is hanging low. The bell has just rung and all the kids, including the kid who smacked the coffee cup out of my hand, are now in class. A few moments ago, my battle-hardened students were reeling back in genuine shock, not even trying to stir a pot so fully mixed. Now, I am alone on a battlefield of linoleum. I haven't moved an inch in the last minute, rock solid like a statue, clearly stunned, and it is very clear to me: I'm in big trouble.

Of course, Andre is in trouble too. He just smacked a coffee cup out of a teacher's hand. That's bad. But it's Mr. Coady who is in real trouble here, and in this sense, Mr. Coady can relate to George Washington.

It's not exactly like watching someone rinse their hands

with someone's brains, but it may be the 2014 public school teacher equivalent of it. And just as George Washington might have miscalculated in attacking a bunch of sleeping Frenchmen in a rainy glen, Mr. Coady laid his foot on a student's boot in what can only be seen as a provocation, however playfully intended. And just as Washington is able to do the math in mere seconds after Jumonville's death, so can Mr. Coady after the smacking of the coffee cup.

How could Mr. Coady have been so stupid?

Every time I've told the story of the coffee cup, I've detected that question lurking a few inches beneath the surface of the listener. At the moment when I describe touching Andre's foot with my boot, a blankness enters the eyes of my audience. They're adopting a neutral pose to cover what they're thinking: *Oh my God, what an idiot!*

But not my wife. She's heard this story a number of times and always stops at this point, plaintively asking, "What the hell were you thinking?"

This is a tough question because the obvious answer is that I wasn't thinking. But this does not satisfy her. She just shakes her head and repeats, "What the hell were you thinking?" Perhaps she has a point. I mean, I must have been thinking something. We've been through this several times over the years, and she always goes on to point out that shoes are kind of a big deal to my students, and I should have known that, and what the hell was I thinking, anyway?

Big deal? For some of my students, it's an addiction. Lila Torres, for example, speaks incessantly about toplines and stitches and turn seams from time to time kicking her own new pair of sneakers off, so she can bring the sole to her nose and take in the bouquet of the fresh rubber. This habit gets stranger when she insists other students lend her their new shoes, so she can take a whiff of their fresh rubber. And while she represents the far extremes of connoisseurship, Andre is a snappy dresser himself, impeccably decked out, and his shoes are pristine.

All of this points to an obvious fact we haven't yet discussed: there is a cultural divide between myself and my students, not to mention the power dynamic and racial issues. I am white; they are Hispanic and Black. I am upper-middle class; they are decidedly not. I might reasonably recognize myself in the power structure of the nation dating back to the Founding Fathers; they have Obama, stuck in the middle of his second term about to become a lame duck.

I carry with me the weight of the system, which includes but is not limited to policemen in the building, administration on every floor, the Massachusetts Department of Elementary and Secondary Education, and policemen on the street. If all else fails, and a revolution is at last at hand, I have the four branches of the United States Armed Forces to protect me. I am also safely ensconced in every social norm available – civic-minded job, modest but solid house, environmentally-friendly hatchback, conscientious and intelligent wife, cute two-year-old at home. Beneath my 20-foot-wide balancing beam, many levels of safety nets are there to catch me if I fall. So yeah, I'm good. No one can touch me.

Or can they? From this description, you might reach the conclusion that I represent "The Man" in the hallway. But that is not wholly accurate, either, and it is certainly not what it feels like. There may be a powerful system running the show, but up here on the fourth floor in a building with no distinguishing marks, it sure feels like the middle of nowhere. I, like many other 9th-grade teachers at Commerce, am barely hanging on. Survival is counted in hours, sometimes minutes. Friday is an achievement, and one of the hardest days of the week, particularly if it coincides with a full moon. Fact.

In every block, teachers are outnumbered. Extract, if you like, the students who "behave" and even the ones not actively looking for trouble, and still the count is ten to one against the teacher. Bell rings, doors close, and now you must contain your students, maybe even teach them. That is the reality of a battle where your chosen career is tested daily, both by the intrinsic desire to persist and the external tasks of not tripping any wires like saying the wrong thing. Or, perhaps, tapping the foot of a student you were just play-boxing.

There is a vast gulf between myself and my students, but it does not take into account that Andre and I are also similar in a number of ways. We're both quick to transgress and test boundaries. We both use humor to get where we're going. We both want to be in charge. We're both interested and invested in tribal culture – Andre and his posse – me and my obsession with organized crime, which almost saw me beaten up when I was in New York (a story for another book).

I have 40 years of Enlightenment-style training and have been taught to prize reason and fairness and institutions, but it's not what I naturally gravitate toward. Actually, I'd rather be with Andre and his crew. I might not like some of the outcomes, and I may not have the willpower to last long, but I envy the strength and immediacy of their relationships.

Maybe Andre sees that potential in me when he comes up and throws mock punches. Maybe that's why I respond to those mock punches by wanting more, eliciting a response from Andre that is strong and immediate and comes perilously close to taking a real punch. Covered in hot coffee wondering how I will keep my job might not be a cozy feeling, but it is vivid, and it does feel real, and it's not something I will soon forget. Obviously.

Now, it's safe to say that this moment from 2014 will not be studied 100 years from now, but let's imagine it is. None of these details will be accounted for. Broad understanding will take the place of thousands of variables, a process of inevitable simplification that will create a rupture between what is represented and what really happened. It will also depend on the politics of the future, how history is viewed, and who it is designed to serve. Too many details will be lost. They will not know that Andre and I were in a good mood that morning, that I was happy to have a free first block, that my intentions were misguided but innocent, or all the other vagaries of our very vague relationship.

Think back on the moment Mark Antony approached Caesar with the gift of the diadem. Yes, it's a few millennia back, but it was also the red-hot center of the known world with the two most powerful men enjoying their moment in the sun. Despite this, we are clueless as to Mark Antony's intentions or what Caesar really thought of the strange episode. No smartphones were handy to record the scene, but boy, those Romans really could talk and write. And still, we are unsure of this moment between the two. That's a shame because it might explain a lot.

Andre and I, on the other hand, are more likely to be buried in our shared anonymity. The building itself seems designed to contain everything that happens inside, and the system is set up to make sure no one outside of the building will be bothered by our lives. It is a fortress of obscurity.

Unlike ancient Rome, our exchange in the hallway exists in a time where all kinds of recording devices are handy – even busy surveillance cameras. However, their records are scrubbed clean by week's end. And I happen to know, for a fact, that no paper trail of the episode exists, and this is very much by design, for both Andre and me. So, if we're trying to understand this moment, we find ourselves at a loss save for one important fact: I was there when it happened.

Which begs the question: What did I do next?

GET RID OF THE EVIDENCE, of course. I get the mop in the hall closet to clean the floor, then go to the bathroom to clean up my shirt. This move has the benefit of calming me down and giving me time to consider my predicament. In the simplest sense, a student just smacked a cup of coffee out of my hand. But we know it is more than that. That I had been playing with Andre, testing him, trying to parlay our lighthearted dance into another round.

And why would I do that? Is it because Coady is just cool like that? Or confused like that? Coady has the boots with the slight toe, the vest, and the paper cup of coffee, not the boring ceramic mug. Coady can mix it up in the hall with his students, ride the line, and come away with the winnings therein. Is that it? Maybe. I don't know. Writing these words, I rack my intact brains with the question my wife puts to me: *What the hell were you thinking?*

I say, "What do you mean? I wasn't thinking."

"No," says my wife. "What the hell were you thinking?"

If nothing else, what comes next is full of thought, mostly of the kind designed to cover my ass.

Andre, myself, and the students who watched us know that Andre's attack, while an overreaction, was not unprovoked and that, as the teacher, the adult, the power in the hall, I should have known better than to cross the line concerning the boots on his feet. And so, there is no prosecution of Andre that should not include the prosecution of myself if I am being honest.

Yes, honest. It is a policy of mine to be honest, even if slight factual shavings might be traced in my wake. Because the benefit of telling the truth is the benefit of not having to keep your story straight. I also believe you should run toward a problem at full speed. Time is of the essence, and the sooner you expose the wound, the easier it can be healed. Because what you must never never, never do is give yourself the time and space to initiate a cover-up.

By the time the coffee is mopped up, a few things are clear: I need to come clean on my part in the exchange while keeping Andre on the hook. His cup smacking is major enough to counterbalance my transgression, and that balance must be maintained throughout. It is also important that Andre be checked for what he has done because I am his teacher, and it is my responsibility to apply some kind of lesson here. This is ethical and unavoidable.

But I also have to consider the wider audience – those shocked kids who watched Andre's attack and then disappeared into the math room when the bell rang. They're in there now, waiting to see what happens next. Will Coady bring down the full force of the law on Andre and have him expelled? Or will Coady let the incident pass to cover his own tracks? Both options will rob me of much-needed credibility with them, and we are only halfway through the year. Mortally wounded by the episode, I may never recover: the temperature and general disorder will rise in every class going forward until late June. Torture.

Besides this, neither of these options would work. Word will get out. It always does. And then there will be questions of why I threw said student under the bus to protect myself or neglected to follow up on a case of such blatant insubordination.

If all of this sounds cynical to you, remember that I am a history teacher. I spend my workdays with Machiavelli, Mao, and Kissinger. Nor do I in general – and specifically here – offer myself up as a role model. My inclination for self-preservation is strong. And you'll pardon me for comparing myself favorably to the Founding Father of our nation, but my next move is one that a young George Washington should have considered in his post-mess-up frenzy: I head straight to my superior to come clean and seek reinforcements.

So, what about our paper cup? Is it still our prop? I picked it up off the floor of the hall, but I didn't throw it out. Instead, I put it in my classroom, over on a sideboard where the heaters are, directly under the window. Evidence, I think lamely. But it will sit there for weeks, warming in the winter sun. I will look at it and consider throwing it away but always stop short. Because now it's a reminder. No, I'm not going to get it bronzed, and it has not quite reached relic status, but it's still more than a used paper cup. It's not trash yet. It's hanging onto its status as a prop.

But interestingly, it may no longer be the principal prop in this story. After all, this is a story about hands but also, importantly, feet. Both Andre and I were wearing boots that day. This is kind of important because Andre was more likely to be wearing sneakers, even in the winter, and there's a difference between sneakers and boots. Boots belong to the adult world, and an attack on them is an attack on manhood in this case.

In a place like Commerce, footwear is the chief indicator of status. Families of students might struggle with any number of expenses, but kids are always geared up with the correct footwear. Electricity and gas might be cut due to unpaid bills, but students wear a couple of hundred dollars on their feet, rotated quarterly. And that's just the way it is. At Commerce, most teachers speak about this dismissively, but these purchases are acts of love and preservation. Overpriced footwear is not a luxury at Commerce; it's a necessity.

And so, while in this book the paper cup takes center stage for reasons of drama, the real prop is probably our boots. My boots were the means by which I might distinguish myself as hip in the world, not just your average teacher stuck in anonymous terrain, but Andre's boots were his national borders. We were both looking to connect that morning, and both of us were projecting meaning into our boots beyond their intended purpose. Alas, I crossed Andre's frontier, and a skirmish began. Now, Andre waits in math class, probably watching the door to see what will happen while Coady scrambles to mop up the mess in the hall and seek out his superior to bury the situation.

One thing I have going for me is Keisha Davis, Assistant Principal for the 9th grade. She is in her first year and is drowning in a torrent of misbehavior. She does not have time for this kind of horseshit. Flying under her radar is not difficult. She wants you to fly under her radar, to do it as politely and discreetly as possible, so she can take care of the 500 other things that cannot be overlooked or kicked under the carpet.

And this is why I enter her office and slip into a chair with as complete a plan as possible. She looks at me expectantly. I'm not a frequent visitor, and she sees I'm in a state. My shirt is stained with coffee, and my eyes flash trouble.

Step one is to explain what Andre did ten minutes ago. This will give her a problem she does not want, so step two must immediately follow: explain the complete sequence of events, including my culpability in the matter, making as full a disclosure as possible without admitting anything that will warrant documentation. It is essential to maintain the position that at most it was an error in judgment, not a deliberate provocation, but that I know it was stupid. This is not as difficult as it is true.

While perhaps she'll be a little confused about what is going on, she may feel relief that my own actions counterbalance Andre's in a way that mitigates the difficulty of dealing with him, especially as he is one of the few students who has an involved parent. Step two is to clarify the issue at hand and offer a solution: while it is likely Andre felt provoked by my error, we obviously cannot let it pass without comment. Step three is to give her the power to make a decision, affirming her role, by requesting that she accompany me to get Andre out of math class, so we can discuss the event.

She agrees. We move down the hall, heading for Andre.

. . .

IMAGINE I have a class in front of me. Not Andre's class and not from that year. A different year, a different school, one with no metal detectors at the entrance. It's sometime in October, right around when we begin to first deal with document-based questions and have to sort through historical sources.

Quite frankly, it's not looking like the best day to do this because it's just after lunch and the kids are wound up – talking loudly, checking their phones, tossing items around the room, or in what is often the best of the worst, slumping with their head face down on their desks. As the bell rings, with no impact on my beloved students, it's clear I'll need to get their attention to proceed.

"You all hear about the fight?" I ask them. Suddenly, they're all ears. Even the heads planted face down on the desks rise up.

"Eighth graders," I say. "It got pretty vicious."

Some kids are halfway out of their seats, as if the fight is still going on and they can rush to check out the scene. They pepper me with names: *Lucas? Sam? Alex?* I deposit these names in my memory bank because the 8th graders will be seated where they are next year, and it's good to know who is in trouble. I may get cute, asking, "Which Sam?" This excites them because there are no more than two or three Sams in the 8th grade. They're getting close.

One student offers, "I saw him running from the courts."

"You saw who?" I ask.

"Sam," says the students.

"Sam who?" another student asks.

"Sam Kotter."

The kids collectively groan. "So what? Sam Kotter is no fighter."

They ask if it's Sam Sadowski, and I just shrug, demurring, which is enough of a confirmation to have them rapidly constructing a narrative. Well, if it's Sam Sadowski, then it's probably a fight with Pete Girand because of what happened last week in P.E.; Sam went up for a jump shot, and Pete pushed him in midair, and Sam got all hot about it.

My students are really getting humming, cranking out all the context necessary for a good fight or even a screenplay. But I have to be careful here. I can't make too many insinuations or let them go into narrative hyperdrive for too long. If I do, the information will jump the boundaries of our classroom, hit the halls (or more likely the Wi-Fi), and be all over school in minutes, leaving one Sam Sadowski puzzled and maybe even a bit offended. Why is his future history teacher implicating him in a fight that did not happen?

Time to pull the plug.

"Whoa, hold up," I say. "There was no fight."

They're stopped cold in their tracks.

"There was no fight," I repeat. "I was making it up."

They should be mad, but it's October, and they know me by now. I've told them not to trust me. *Never trust your history teacher.* Besides, I've given them the adrenaline rush a real fight would have provided. Still aglow with the excitement of imagining Sam and Lenny going toe to toe, perhaps hoping for an afterschool rematch, they chastise me for being deceitful but do so gently.

"But if there was a fight," I continue, "Who would you want to ask about it?"

"Sam," says one student.

"Hold on," I say, "Forget about Sam and Pete, I don't want that getting around the school." They laugh at the prospect. "But you're saying you'd go to someone who was in the fight, right? Okay, but what's the problem with that?"

It takes them a minute, and they need a little coaxing, but they come to the conclusion that, while there are some things that are useful about going to one of the fighters, there are also a lot of limitations, including their obvious bias and the fact that were probably so worked up they're not necessarily going to have a good recollection of the events. So, who else?

"Maybe a friend who is nearby," a student offers.

"A friend of yours or a friend of the fighters?"

"I don't know, maybe both. Sam's a friend of mine."

"Oh geez, forget about Sam, will you? What's the problem with going to one of the friends of the fighters?"

Bias, they say. Yes, *bias*. So, you can go to the fighters, even the friends of the fighters, but that might not be your best source.

And so, who might be better? A teacher, maybe?

No way, they say, teachers never know what's going on.

Okay, how about someone quiet who was there but isn't

friends with either of the fighters? It might be someone kind of anonymous, right?

"Maybe," they say, "it depends on the person."

I agree. "Right, it depends on the person."

I'VE TALKED about my encounter with Andre many times over the years, but it is only now, writing about it as a piece of history in this book, that it occurs to me that my own understanding might be limited if not flat-out wrong.

Part of the problem is that I've built this story up over the years. It's a moment I "remember" so vividly that I am able to slow down, rewind, and replay each step of the way projected in high definition on the back of the inside of my skull. And the more I think about it, the more definite it gets – which is, in itself, a problem with history. If we invest in it, we intend to live in it, and its structural integrity must always be shored up lest it be questioned. Because it is ours.

But it is not just mine. Andre must have his own memory of it, as do the other students who were surrounding us and even the kids down the hall who only caught a glimpse of it. Miguel Martinez was right there, next to us. What did he think happened? How about Jayden Wright? Jayden was there, too. What did people who were not in the hall hear about it? Could they possibly remember after all these years now passed? After all, they didn't get doused in coffee, and the High School of Commerce certainly did not lack competing plot lines.

What about Andre? Does he remember the coffee cup? How much of what he remembers matches my recollections? Does he remember the play boxing we did before the incident? Was he really mad about my foot hitting his boots, or was it a calculated response? How about the talk with Principal Davis and myself? Was Andre able to hear our little talk? Did it help? Did he sense I was trying to cover my backside? What about Miguel and Jayden? They were next to us. What understanding could they bring to the table that might inch us a little closer to what actually happened in that anonymous hallway?

Time to find Miguel and Jayden. Time to find Andre.

6

PAPIER MÂCHÉ

21 PRAIRIAL 1794

It's June 8th, or 20 Prairial, also known as the day of Fourche, or pitchfork. Because all the days have names now. This is 1794, by the way, unless you're in revolutionary France, in which case it is year two. Just so you don't get confused, the weeks now have ten days, which is actually meant to confuse you, especially if you're religious and are trying to locate the sabbath, which is expressly forbidden anyway, so rest assured this confusion is being generated for your own safety.

This new revolutionary calendar is just another piece of great reform for the overgrown and insect-infested garden of France; though, it does have an unresolved issue with leap years. This almost gets solved when Gilbert Romme suggests years IV, VIII, XII, and so forth include an extra day with the exception of year 4000, which is 3998 years away.

Unfortunately, Romme is sentenced to the guillotine for non-leap-year-related charges, a fate he escapes by stabbing himself multiple times on the staircase outside a court, declaring, "I die for the republic!" Fortunately, the republic he dies for only lasts until 11 Frimaire, the day of Cire, or wax, Year XIII, or 2 December 1804.

Anyway, it's the day of the Pitchfork, or 20 Prairial, which is the Month of the Meadow, in year 2, or June 8, 1794, which happens to be the day of Pentecost on the Old Gregorian calendar. Though, we probably shouldn't say that – *or even think it* – because Christianity has been outlawed here.

Fortunately, it just so happens to be the perfect kind of day to start a cult. We are in Paris, France, which happens to be a very culty place, and we are in the throes of the really fun part of the revolution known as the Great Terror when guillotine blood streams down cobblestones and pools in front of cafes and gets so smelly that croissant hawkers are basically like, "Hey, all this blood is totally stinking up the place and driving away my customers. Any chance we can give another neighborhood a chance to host the National Razor?" And the officials are like, "Sure, makes sense. We'll move the guillotine to another avenue."

Wow, that's what I call responsive, egalitarian governance!

It's a beautiful morning, 20 Prairial, year two. I'm not going to try to determine the hour because days in the new calendar have ten hours with 100 minutes, only they're not really minutes because they have 100 decimal seconds.

The sun is up, the sky is blue, fluffy clouds are floating cheerfully in the air, and there's barely a pitchfork or sharp object in sight. Even the guillotine is given the day off, which is cause for some relaxing celebration; though, many are aware that the head-chopping business will be back in operation tomorrow, which is probably why their celebrations are so earnestly on display and perhaps not so relaxing at all. Everyone hangs tricolor banners from their windows and hustles down to the street to march around the city, smiles plastered to their faces.

To be fair, plenty of people actually are having a great time because no one enjoys marching under empty ideological banners more than the French. Parisians, in particular, join parades, processions, and protests the way middle-aged middle managers from middle America enjoy the middle of golf courses.

Paris is filled with banks of roses and young women in white dresses. Eight oxen with their horns painted gold are pulling a cart carrying a printing press and a plow, which is kind of like the sickle and hammer before the sickle and hammer existed. Another cart has blind children singing a Hymn to Divinity, and that is followed by mothers carrying roses, which is followed by fathers leading their sons, who are equipped with swords. There's a cardboard statue with donkey ears that no one can quite figure out, but its purpose will become clear later when it gets engulfed in flames.

But the pièce de résistance is a *papier-mâché* mountain in the Champ de la Réunion. It's quite impressive, a man-made mini mountain, 40 feet from top to bottom, complete with a tree on top. There are platforms and walkways, and any reasonable Parisian might wonder where the money is coming from to build it, but a smart Parisian would not actually ask this question out loud.

Befitting a set of this size, there is a chorus of 2,400 singers, belting out such catchy lines as, "*The august freedom, the scourge of perverts,*" and "*The temple is on the mounts, in the air, on the waves,*" and hit-making refrains like, "*More lethal than tyrants! More lethal than tyrants!*" No doubt it will be the song of the summer, particularly amongst those notorious party people, the Jacobins.

Speaking of which, look there, on top of the mountain, it's an all-around good guy and resident madman Maximilien Robespierre. He's Jacobin #1 and the head of the Committee of Public Safety, whose job is to keep the public safe by making the public fear for their safety. He's become associated with purges and the national razor, blood-stained baskets, and decapitated heads. But worry not because today is the Festival of the Supreme Being, and he couldn't be happier. He's bringing virtue to the masses and imbuing the Republic with magical powers to create long-term unity. It's his crowning achievement. He's not here to condemn hundreds of people to death; he's here to party hard. He is actually wearing a toga and is now descending down the *papier-mâché* mountain.

Now, remember, this is the Festival of the Supreme Being, and here's a toga-clad Robespierre stepping down from great heights, divinely framed by a blue sky and puffy clouds. It's kind of hard not to do the math on this one, folks, and sure enough, some of the crowd's rougher elements, not content to leave well enough alone, begin pointing out the obvious: "Look, he thinks he's a new God!"

It's not just one person, either. It's a number of them from tough-talking sans-culottes to book-smart rivals of Robespierre. Here he is, half-naked in a toga atop a *papier-mâché* mountain surrounded by a chorus of 2,400 singing about tyrants and trying to pass himself off as a God on Earth. Worse, it ain't working.

What a complete and total narcissistic tool.

I'M afraid I owe Maximilien Robespierre an apology. I fear this for two reasons: for one, I am no fan of Robespierre and having to double back and cough up an apology to an unapologetic tyrant is a bit of a drag.

Secondly, Robespierre does not have the best reputation when it comes to accepting apologies. He's a bit of a crybaby, really quite paranoid on balance, and lightning-quick to take offense. He's also an ideological fanatic from hell. Altogether, it's not a great combination, fusing personal frailty with a world-historical vision that leaves little wriggle room for mercy. When you have erred against Robespierre, you have erred against the Revolution – no, not just the Revolution – *against the course of inevitable human evolution.*

Yikes. And I thought stepping on Andre's boot might get me in trouble.

Perhaps you think the fact that Robespierre has been dead for more than two centuries would keep me safe, but sadly, this is not the case. Because in terms of reputation, Max is very much alive and unwell. His legacy is so disputed by historians that you can almost smell his fetid, decomposing body being run up and down the field of inquiry – supporters propping up his corpse – detractors trying to bury him again. Fortunately for me, the aghast members of the faculty won't notice me here at the university gates with my organ grinder and monkey on a leash attracting the lumpen mass (you!) for my spiel.

But yes, an apology is owed to Robespierre the Incorruptible. For one, and it pains me to admit this, Robespierre was *not* wearing a toga atop his *papier-mâché* mountains. It's such a great detail and goes such a long way with my students that I have used it for years and am loath to let go of it – I even used it for a period after I found out it was not true. No one is sure of the origin of the toga myth; although, Robespierre had actually been seen in a toga a number of times. But alas, no, at this event Maximilien is looking sharp in a blue coat and a giant tri-color sash, pretty much standard fare for an event like this.

In terms of factual veracity, there is another issue going on here, and in this case, the apology might be owed to you, my reader. The title of this chapter is *Papier Mâché*, and it is a reference to the mountain constructed in the middle of Paris, the one that Robespierre descends NOT dressed in a toga. While this mountain is constructed in the same manner as a *papier-mâché* model, it is durable plaster that serves as the shell around the wooden scaffolding.

This substitution has been a conscious deceit on my part as there are many reasons why this chapter needs to be called *papier mâché*, not the least that *papier* will play a major role in two incidents that follow the Festival of the Supreme Being. As we shall see, the event on the mountain is more of an odd pit-stop, a one-off in the revolution. The really bad stuff awaits. So, while, like Caesar, I am happy to discard the toga, I cling tightly to the *papier mâché*.

The other odd item on this chapter's title page is the date I have selected. Did you notice it or blow right by it? If not, go back and check it out. For French Revolutionary buffs out there, 21 Prairial is an odd choice. Nothing happened on 21 Prairial, so it is an odd choice. And important. *And...*

Perhaps, I am simply procrastinating because my real apology to Robespierre has yet to be tendered. Dressing him in a toga like a doll for the amusement of my students is historical chump change, small-scale chicanery to get the attention of students who might have spent the last block running in circles or studying fallopian tubes, hopefully not at the same time.

But presenting Robespierre as a delusional God descending from the heavens, while a compelling image, is quite inaccurate. Worse, it is really unfair because, at the very moment that Robespierre appears to be his most narcissistic, monomaniacal, psychotic worst, he is actually, improbably, at his most tolerant, reasonable, generous best.

Oh, history. What a bitch.

. . .

As we look at history through a pair of backward binoculars, events and people become greatly reduced. If nothing else, it makes it easy to get a handle on them and fold them in our social wallets as we make our way through college parties, singles mixers, weddings, and funerals.

Robespierre somehow (don't ask me how) comes up in conversation, and we have a brief Wikipedia entry's worth of him stored in our cranial drive, just enough to get through the conversation and not embarrass ourselves or anyone else. Robespierre means fanatic, far left, perpetrator of the Great Terror. Maybe, if we're running with a bookish crowd or suddenly develop a fetish for Marxists, we know more: Robespierre = Jacobin, head of the Committee of Public Safety, killer of Danton, ironically shot his own jaw off just before ironically getting his head chopped off on the instrument he wielded so deftly, the guillotine.

Anything beyond that and we run the risk of being a pompous know-it-all, of producing the exact opposite effect from what we intended, driving attractive people to the other end of the bar in a search for genial, less Robespierre-obsessed company. Believe me, I know.

While it is easy to see Robespierre simply as a radical, as the man who outflanked the left to get the furthest left and dumped the revolution into a blood-stained basket, it's actually not that accurate. In fact, there were plenty of impassioned factions running around Paris looking to force their agendas into the power vacuum left behind by the Ancient Regime. As noted before, nothing excites a Parisian more than a banner with a slogan, and some of these groups are even more radical, even more fanatic, and even more annoyingly bloodthirsty than our friend Maximilien Robespierre and his Jacobin pals.

Like Jacques Hébert, for example. Though his background mirrors Robespierre in its privilege and education, Hébert is more adept at playing the street thug, writing articles in his newspaper with the *nom de plume* Père Duchesne, adopting the voice of a rough *sans-culotte*, and really letting fly. If that sounds like a shameless piece of slumming to you, then we agree. But it is also a fantastic hit as most displays of shamelessness are. "The Homer of filth," as one historian called him, Hébert rarely fails to feed the angry flames in the poorer parts of Paris while calling for the death of all aristocrats. And priests.

Yup, he's a straight-up atheist. He is dedicating his life to not believing in God. This is a reasonable choice, though one I've found befuddling. After all, how would it be possible to know there is no God unless you are all-powerful and thus God? I suppose, like a good Catholic, it can be a belief based on faith – faith that the universe is a frightening, empty void. But hey, to each their own. A sentiment that the atheist in question, Jacques Hébert, does not share.

To call him "intolerant" would be an understatement. Hébert, and like-minded folk in the dechristianization crowd, went on the offensive in 1793. They execute hundreds of priests, exile tens of thousands more, close churches, outlaw worship, and smash religious statuary. Active priests, and anyone harboring them, can be killed on the spot. Priests are forced to renounce their faith or prematurely meet the maker they are faithful to, a strange bind. Some priests are even forced to get married. Again, a strange bind but one with a few more clear upsides.

And then, just to make the whole dechristianization kick official, Hébert and his pals decide to have a festival. Because what's a homicidal, debasing, inhumane pogrom without a party to celebrate it? They're going to call it the Festival of Reason, and it predates the Festival of the Supreme Being by eight months. They replace Catholic altars in churches with Altars of Reason and place signs above cemeteries reading, "Death is an eternal sleep."

Wow, isn't that just a super great reminder? So helpful. Thanks, guys.

Reading accounts of the event from the time, the festival sounds like a script from a pornographic movie; though, many of these accounts are probably exaggerated. They did use live women to replace the idolatry of statuary, and in Paris, that means Sophie Momoro, wife of one of Hébert's collaborators, plays the part of the Goddess of Reason. She dresses provocatively and (allegedly) receives worshippers of reason with an intimate kiss. Her teeth aren't great, but this otherwise sounds rather agreeable. Unless you're Maximilien Robespierre, who needs to be the center of everything and is also a bit of a prig.

In fact, he is disgusted. The kissing is the least of it. For while he is suspicious of priests, as he is suspicious of every other living being, he is not actually for dechristianization. He believes it will alienate neutral powers and the French masses, leading to the Civil War. He believes that pure atheism is elitist, a tiny club of smug nihilists out of touch with the common man. He may not believe in God, but he believes in atheism even less. Nor does it help that the followers of Hébert have coalesced to the point where they begin calling themselves Hébertist, a moniker only a French person could walk around calling themselves with a straight face. And so, all the elements are in place: a disagreeable notion, promiscuous kissing, a rising faction, and a ridiculous name. We're definitely in France.

After the Hébertists overstep and attempt a failed revolt, Robespierre makes quick work of them, staging their trial and execution all in a couple of hours (bearing in mind that hours had 100 decimal minutes back then, and minutes had 100 decimal seconds – I can't really figure it out, but it's quick). And then, just to make the whole widespread destruction of the Hébertists official, they decide to have a festival. Because what's a homicidal, debasing, inhumane pogrom without a party to celebrate it?

They're going to call it the Festival of the Supreme Being.

So, let's go find our pal Robespierre where we left him. He's up on the plaster mountain in his big sash framed by blue skies and puffy clouds. This is the Festival of the Supreme Being, the inaugural event of the Cult of the Supreme Being, and here he is, seemingly presenting himself as that Supreme Being. And that's just really awkward for everyone, particularly Robespierre, and although he might have been smart and anticipated this error, it is just that, an error.

What Robespierre is trying – *trying* – to do with his Cult of the Supreme Being is to inject some virtue into the Revolution. He is aware that a society without a coalescing virtuous core will fall into ruin, and he is worried that the Revolution has swung too far into radical nihilism under Hébertist influence. He is in no position to reinstate the Catholic Church of course, nor does he want to. He can imagine true freedom of worship somewhere down the line, but it won't do for now. At the same time, the French need a unifying force, something more than just the machinations of change to inspire them. Because there are just so many times you can sing the Marseillaise before you want to shoot yourself in the face.

And so, he does what any self-respecting child of the Enlightenment might do. He seeks to create an organization at the center of society defined vaguely enough so that multiple viewpoints about it can peacefully coexist. This is one of the main aims of the Enlightenment: to reduce tribalism by creating shared institutions. It may not have the potency and focus of a belief system like Catholicism, but it is more inclusive, trading intensity for coexistence.

On the day of the Festival of the Supreme Being, looking up at that fake mountain with the real blue sky and puffy clouds behind it, you can project whatever you like upon its splendor. For you, "Reason" might be your Supreme Being, and that's what you worship. But you are shoulder to shoulder with your fellow Parisians, and the person standing next to you might gaze up that mountain and imagine "God" – as in the Christian God – is their Supreme Being. And then you can all do what the French people do best, which is drink wine and eat cheese and complain about how bad the guillotine blood stinks in this part of town.

Indeed, Robespierre's speech from atop the mountain is blisteringly vague. There are theist overtones aplenty, but they move around like a net being angled to capture the maximum number of souls. In addition to speaking about a Supreme Being, he drops the following names: God, Divinity, Creator of Nature, Great Being, and Being of Beings. That's a whole lot of Beings, and hopefully, one of them can work for you, sparking your own projection upon the mountain. You can then commence to mellow out with some wine, remember this festival fondly, and hopefully – *maybe* – be a little bit more virtuous in the coming year. If nothing else, you might remember the cardboard statue with the donkey ears that went up in flames in a most righteous and bright fashion. And do you know what the statue represented? Hideous Atheism. So good, we're done with that.

There's only one problem with all of this. Despite the intentions behind this spectacle, the optics look bad. It's hard to get past the obvious. Toga or not, the fact that Robespierre is pontificating vaguely about beings atop the mountain surrounded by puffy clouds and a chorus of 2,400 leaves him open, at the very least, to accusations that he is passing himself off as that Supreme Being. And that is why all these years later, this generally terrible human being still provides some comic relief to my classroom of high school students. We can delight in a chuckle at his expense and go home and tell our parents the fun fact in Coady's class as Robespierre writhes in his grave. I'd feel bad about this if I didn't think he deserved to do a little bit of eternal writhing in his grave.

Interestingly, there is another reason why Robespierre might have looked as if he were passing himself off as a living Supreme Being. At one point, as the procession is about to move forward, the other members of the convention, whether on purpose or not, pause where they are, which leaves Robespierre standing alone front and center. This is not in the script, and I've seen it referred to as a prank. The other Revolutionaries are having a bit of fun at Robespierre's expense.

Pardon me, but it's hard for me to accept it as a joke because this is decidedly not the pranking kind of crowd. They're chopping heads off to punish the sale of bad wine and conducting bat-crap crazy reorganizations of the calendar. It's easier to see the pause as merely accidental, the kind of screw-up that happens all the time with processions. Or one might, if they're the paranoid kind, even see it as a kind of sabotage, "Here, it's Maxie's festival. He wants it so bad. Let him own it for good or for bad." Knowing Robespierre, regardless of the intent behind it, it's hard to imagine his receiving it as a prank or an accident, and it's much more likely he'd see it as an act of subterfuge.

Whatever the case, Robespierre goes first, which puts him

very much out in the open, vulnerable to a number of taunts coming out of the massive crowd. Drunk *sans-culottes* and rival faction leaders can use the relative anonymity of the crowd to take their potshots at the incorruptible. He's called a tyrant and a dictator by a select few, including convention heavies like Thirion and Ruamps. There are a few thinly veiled threats of assassination. And then of course, there's the smart aleck *sans-culottes* who gives voice to what a lot of people are likely thinking, "Look at him – he thinks himself a God!"

Does it phase him? Hard to say, really. Robespierre hears the slanders, and he's a sensitive soul, but this is not the first time he's been roughed up by a crowd. Moreover, the festival is a big hit among the people and a major achievement. Parisians like processions and ox-drawn carts and plaster mountains. Plenty of them can gaze upon the summit of that pretend mountain, taking in Robespierre's vague declarations, and find their own Supreme Being. And it's not just in Paris. Festivals are successfully held all over the country.

It's an impressive feat, both logistically and ideologically. Robespierre and company have turned a corner for the Revolution, injecting a necessary dose of communal virtue, quieting the nihilistic atheist crowd, and bringing a newfound unity that is distinct and more elevated than the day-to-day struggle of bloody trials and bloody Austrians looming on the bloody borders.

In fact, to hear many around him say it was the happiest

day in Robespierre's life. All of which really begs the question: why the hell did what come next, come next?

21 Prairial passes without incident.

22 Prairial, however, does not. It is the day of Chamomile, an herb that has calmed billions of people over the ages. Unfortunately, for the French, the day of Chamomile will have the exact opposite effect, producing the Law of 22 Prairial, which has the dubious distinction of being the foundational document for modern totalitarianism. In this sense, it might be the deadliest piece of *papier* in history, not so much due to its local impact on 1794 France as its historical reach. Diligent students of terror like Stalin and Mao, so eager to learn how to subjugate the masses, await down the road to inherit its bone-crushing guidance.

For one, slandering the Republic, or even failing to adequately support it, can lead to charges, as can demonstrating depraved morals or reporting fake news. And who is to decide which news is fake and which news is real? Trials are limited to three days, which actually ends up being more like three hours. Revolutionary tribunals cannot call witnesses, and defendants are also refused the right to counsel, forcing juries to decide the fates of the accused based on the charges and their own defense. The only permissible verdicts are total acquittal or total death. Examining these factors, it is easy to see how many jurors might favor the latter. It is so much easier to resolve the issue permanently than to face the prospect of a person going free only to come back to haunt your verdict. You might end up in the same predicament with a risk-averse jury thinking the very same thing.

In the defense of the law, there is a legitimate issue facing the Revolution: the prisons are overflowing. Naturally, you don't want to leave your opponents out running on the field when faced with an existential crisis, but you also need to keep count of how many you stuff behind bars as the jails themselves can become hotbeds of revolt. Nor does it help that Paris demands that prisoners in the provinces be sent to the capital to ensure proper oversight, which generally means proper execution. And that would be fine in theory, except that the wheels of injustice are moving much too slowly to clear these prisons out.

Basically, the Law of 22 Prairial, which seems draconian and a bit problematic from a moral, legal, and ethical standpoint, is really a practical step to resolve a pressing issue. Rushed trials and quick executions free up space and eliminate dissent. However, paradoxically, the law actually exacerbates overcrowding because it sets the conditions for hyper paranoia and mass incarceration. As it states, "Every citizen is empowered to seize conspirators and counterrevolutionaries." This opens the doors for tattletales with petty grudges to exact revenge on everyone in sight. Worse, citizens are required to turn in traitors as soon as they know of their existence, making it a civil responsibility to denounce your fellow man. Folks, once these kinds of shenanigans start, they're very hard to stop as regular people reach the terrible conclusion: *Wow, everyone is denouncing each other, and here I am denouncing nobody. I better do something about that.* So, if the point of the law is to empty the jails, it certainly fails at that.

Importantly, the law also removes immunity for members of the Convention. So now the paranoia on the street is the paranoia in government seats. What before might have been a question of debate, now has become a life-and-death struggle. Silence may take the place of dissent, but the dissent is still there. It is, in fact, growing deeper and wider by the hour as those who feel they are a target seek a rapid change in the status quo. The Reign of Terror morphs into the Great Terror, as if this miserable period in history needed an additional honorific.

One of the great ironies is that the Festival of the Supreme Being led many to hope that the Revolution had turned a corner, and that Robespierre might have been willing to mothball the Committee of Public Safety and stem the terror. Blood might stop flowing over cobblestones; the rancid smell of traitors might finally dissipate. France is, after all, no longer in mortal danger from foreign powers, and the Cult of the Supreme Being is viewed as a compromise with people's need to connect with forces more powerful than liberty and equality, offering tolerance and inviting unity. The hideous atheists have been run out of Paris – or actually, Planet Earth

– along with the recently departed Dantonists, and factionalism has relaxed.

Besides, remember, the festival is the happiest day in Robespierre's life, despite the taunts he endures. It's been his dream to bring virtue to the Revolution; although, only two days later, he is devoid of it. He has made a career of denouncing tyrants, and here he is, surpassing all of them in his wickedness. Less than 48 hours after basking in the glow of the communal spirit, he pushes through a law that will effectively snuff it out. This really begs the question: what happened between the festival on 20 Prairial and the Law on 22 Prairial? How did the Revolution go from sweetness and light to sourness and slaughter with such alacrity? How do we resolve this contradiction, this sinister pirouette?

What the hell happened on 21 Prairial?

BEFORE WE DIVE IN, let's look at a few factors dating further back. For one, there have been recent assassination attempts on Robespierre. Two, to be exact, only "exact" is not all that exact in this case because neither of them is all that exacting.

The first is a man hanging around in the street hoping to get a shot at the Incorruptible. Not having the same fortune as Gavrilo Princip later experiences in Sarajevo, he takes a potshot at another member of the Committee of Public Safety instead. His gun misfires, and he is tackled by a locksmith. All in all, it's a pretty lame way to find your head locked in the lunette of a guillotine.

Nonetheless, it pales in comparison to the sad case of Cécile Renault, who shows up at Robespierre's house with hopes of seeing a tyrant in the flesh. She mumbles incoherently and is discovered to be carrying a fruit knife, which is a pretty effective means of killing a piece of brie but not a human being. Nonetheless, she will be executed alongside her family, presumably for providing her with the fruit knife.

It is easy to see how these attempts might connect to the Law of 22 Prairial, and it is true that Robespierre seizes upon them for personal gain. He also seems to legitimately work himself into a hysterical froth regarding his personal safety, but this is hard for me to gauge as I am neither a fanatic nor French. Of course, we know that Robespierre the Incorruptible is highly paranoid, but there are also reports that he is flattered to be considered worth killing. Many times, he's been on the other end of that equation, railing against the impressive danger of the Danton and Hérbert advocating for death to counter their influence. As these assassinations are far from successes, Robespierre is allowed to sniff the hemlock, enjoying its pungent bouquet but not its lethal bite.

So, we are no closer to trying to understand 21 Prairial. And you won't find any answers in the many history books about the French Revolution. Most people would take that as a sure sign that nothing of significance happened on that day, but we are not "most people." We are bold and brave and believe that sometimes, under the camouflage of omission, the real story lies untold.

Fortunately, we live in a world where you can reach out to

famous historians with a simple email, and unbelievably, they usually reply. Perhaps this is due to the relatively small followings afforded famous historians. Getting feedback on 21 Prairial is a lot easier than emailing Taylor Swift your latest song with hopes of being asked to be her next tour opener.

Hervé Leuwers, President of the Society of Robespierrist Studies, will get back to you quickly and even send you the pertinent passage of his book. So will Colin Jones, who wrote the lauded, *The Fall of Robespierre: 24 Hours in Revolutionary Paris*. Incidentally, I also contacted the author of an article posted on Marxist.org (.org, *not* .com) trying to find the origin of this compelling quote they ascribed to Robespierre: "The fall of factions sets all vices free." Alas, they weren't able to locate it, which is a shame because it's a fascinating notion and would have helped this book a lot. Oh, Marx, you've let me down again.

Perhaps because he is a French, and thus better able to gauge Robespierre's disposition, Hervé Leuwers responded to my query by saying he places a lot of emphasis on the assassination attempts. Halfhearted as they might seem to our modern eye, at the time they represent dangers to the Revolution and not just domestically. Robespierre and his clique imagine the hand of England directing these assassination attempts.

Seen this way, the Law of 22 Prairial represents righteous anger against foreign intriguers. As it states in the law itself, "The rule of judgments is the conscience of the jurors enlightened by love of the homeland; their goal, the triumph of the republic, and the ruin of its enemies." Enlightenment? Triumph? Love? These sentiments are indeed consistent with the Festival of the Supreme Being, a world of good and evil. But let's admit it, it's a tough kind of love.

Author Colin Jones also responded to my email, and like Leuwers, he sees Robespierre as trapped by his own dualistic worldview. His veneration for the virtues of the festival is one side of the coin; his contempt for those who would challenge the revolution is the other. Opponents are the enemies of the universal good, and this universal good is so necessary that it needs to be eliminated to protect it. Moreover, Jones postulates that it is actually the success of the festival that emboldens Robespierre. Max takes it as a sign that terror should not abate, but accelerate, as the people have apparently come together to accept his vision and insist that the mission be carried out, no matter the cost.

So, while the celebrants of the festivals might have thought it the end of the hard times, their enjoyment of the day only signaled the opposite to Robespierre. It is a good example of the price of fear – of how when people are oppressed communication breaks down. Veneration and terror are simply two instruments from the same toolbox. It is only we, separated by time and not fanatics by nature, who fail to see this consistency in Robespierre's wicked position.

Ultimately, these historians posit there is no contradiction between the Robespierre of the Festival of the Supreme Being and the Robespierre of the Law of 22 Prairial. They are one and the same. It is only those of us praying for a soft landing for the Revolution and rooting for a Robespierre that is digestible and agreeable who are confused and want to know what happens on 21 Prairial. 21 Prairial is just another day, passing without incident. Robespierre awakens, eats, and sleeps again. And when he next awakens, he pushes through a law that has the same purity of vision as the Cult of the Supreme Being.

This consistency is what makes Robespierre terrifying, a menace the centuries cannot contain. Nothing we can do will give him the purity he seeks. He is the father who cannot accept us, the tyrant who cannot be placated, the wielder of terror whose appetite only increases. Try as we might to find a reason, to revisit 21 Prairial and stalk him during the course of his day, we come back with nothing. He can never be completely laid to rest, and we can never be free. Robespierre is not done with us. Robespierre will never be done with us.

Nor are we done with him.

HIS PROBLEMS BEGIN SHORTLY after the passage of 22 Prairial when he makes an interesting choice: he disappears for a month. There is some evidence of him sporadically working on the Committee of Public Safety in the first few weeks, but after that, he fully disappears. Perhaps his recent brush with death, matched with the knowledge of how many loose fruit knives are scattered across Paris, makes Robespierre err on the side of caution.

But err he does. Because when he leaves the scene, he

creates a vacuum of power with a particularly strong suck. The Law of 22 Prairial has exposed members of the Convention to trial and execution, injecting fear in the arena, and now, with Robespierre absent, factions can form. He lays sick in bed with a fever of his own making, a hypochondriacal extension of his own fanaticism. He offers melancholy musing about the future of the revolution and his own place in it. Meanwhile, members of the Convention are conspiring to keep Robespierre on his back, or even turn his sickness into death.

The art of going missing is one of the not-so-secret themes of this book. Caesar hid in his palace on the Ides of March only to be lured out by a piece of lowly man-shaming. He wouldn't have been much better off living with a bruised ego than dying from 23 stab wounds. After the Diet of Worms, Frederick the Wise stuffs Martin Luther in a drafty castle in Wartburg. It seems like a wise choice until it is not. Chaos breaks out in his absence, and Luther must be recalled to quell the dissent. The Half King, bailing on a flailing George Washington, goes into a self-imposed exile, which is a smart choice. However, it will only keep him going a little further. He dies of sickness shortly thereafter, the ultimate strategy for going missing.

Look, if I had that many daggers pointed at me, I might want to go missing, too. But while it is natural to want to take a break, doing so comes with its own dangers. One of the hardest parts of power is presenting yourself to the public, offering a fleshy target for your enemies to erase. Whether you survive these precarious showings depends on your power base and on millions of miscellaneous factors, the thin space between obsequious grins and razor-sharp whispers. If many supporting factors are in place, you can present yourself with crowns of jewels on your head, and no one will make a move for it. But if your constituency collapses, whispers will turn into daggers strapped to hips, hidden by togas. Nothing will keep you safe in open spaces or closed ones. Of course, the alternative is to be absent altogether, which works so long as you are willing to do it permanently. This, understandably, Robespierre will not do.

He returns to the Convention on 8 Thermidor to give a long, boring, vapid, cliché-ridden speech that invokes just about every empty slogan you can stand. It's a terrific barrage of "friends of liberties" and "henchmen of tyranny," all delivered with requisite passion. Despite the bone-crushing banality, the speech itself is no crime and probably isn't the worst way to reinsert yourself into the dull mass of revolutionary groupthink. What comes next, however, will be a crime, a self-inflicted wound from which Robespierre will not recover.

And now we have reached our third piece of *papier*, one which is, more than any other item in this book, except maybe the forthcoming chalk, undoubtedly a prop. The *papier-mâché* mountain, as we know, is actually made of plaster, and the Law of 22 Prairial, while being a piece of *papier*, is certainly no prop. It might be leverage; it might be a sinister mechanism, but it is no prop. But as Robespierre tediously continues to declaim liberty. He has, in his hand, his final piece of *papier*. Perhaps he feels he's losing the attention of the Convention, or maybe he is just falling back on some of his classic moves. Whatever the case, he waves the piece of *papier* and says, "Will we denounce the traitors?"

Ah, yes, the traitors. Enemies, imagined and real, have been a useful go-to for Robespierre, a track that DJ Maxie can spin anytime the dance floor begins to lag. He has a piece of *papier* in his hand, and he's talking about traitors, so it'd be quite logical to infer that on this piece of *papier* there is a list of traitors. And who are these traitors? Well, that's anyone's guess, really. We don't actually know what is on the piece of *papier* Robespierre is whipping around in the air. What we do know is that it could be basically anyone in the room. And these people in the room have been stewing in the broth of the Law of 22 Prairial for a month. Not only are their antennas up, but they are positively vibrating with anxiety. They look up at Robespierre and the *papier* and ask themselves the inevitable.

Is he talking about me?

Now, I'd like to think that this book offers opportunities for self-improvement. History, while not predictable or sensible, can be useful, mostly for instructing us on what *not* to do. For example, if you ever find yourself sitting in front of the Temple of Goddess Venus and are approached by a long column of senators bearing honors for you, for Chrissakes, stand up when they arrive, you lazy bastard.

Or, if you're scouting enemy positions and come across a

bunch of rifles stacked outside of tents in a rainy glen, consider that their mission may be diplomatic in nature, and it may be prudent to withdraw. Oh yeah, and don't build forts in low-lying meadows that have streams, unless you're 100% certain it will never – *not once* – rain while you remain there.

These lessons have practical applications for you, the reader. You can thank me later when you're lording over your empire. Recall me fondly, and sally forth a bit of coinage for your humble servant.

To that end, let me offer this: if you ever find yourself before an assembled group of fellow revolutionaries – highly paranoid revolutionaries – revolutionaries who are seriously wondering if they might die in the next calendar day – do not, whatever you do, wave around a piece of *papier* vaguely saying you have a bunch of names who are enemies of the revolution.

Because you know what will happen? *Everyone* – every. last. single. paranoid. revolutionary. soul in the room – will plausibly jump to the conclusion that you are talking about *them*. And now, you have assembled a crowd facing an existential problem: *You! You,* Robespierre, are their existential problem!

Do we stay silent and cross our fingers that we're not on Maxie's list and see if we're slated to die? Or do we do something else?

Guess what? We do something else.

The next day members of the Convention moved to arrest Robespierre. Unfortunately, no jail in Paris is willing to contain him, fearing reprisals should he survive the episode. Because he is a survivor. Robespierre ends up at the Hôtel de Ville until 10 Thermidor when rival members of the convention storm, which is something the French like to do almost as much as protest.

In the melee, Robespierre either shoots his own jaw loose or has it shot off for him. Either way, it is bandaged to his head as he is carted away for a trial that is perfectly suited for his present condition: with a jaw hanging loosely from his head he cannot speak, and as a subject of Law of 22 Prairial, he is not really allowed to anyway. Behold the glorious irony. He must endure the system he has put in place, all without the advantage of his eloquent fury. As a comeuppance for a historical figure, this must be in the top ten, maybe even the top three.

He is tried, convicted, thrown in a cart, and sent forthwith to the guillotine.

As a casual observer of the French Revolution, I've always taken Robespierre's nickname, the Incorruptible, to be ironic. Because obviously, despite his good intentions, he is corrupted by his power, right? All his hopes and visions about a virtuous republic are squandered in a paranoid bloodletting that can only end with the letting go of his own blood. Right?

Not necessarily. If we pull out the dictionary, we find the word incorruptible has two definitions. The first is someone who cannot be perverted or bribed. It is fairly certain Robespierre was never successfully bribed, and it's even possible he was never perverted. Robespierre's vices were his own, ever apparent, and did not change.

Knowing this, you can see what an attractive leader Robespierre must have been for his high-flying, high-strung Jacobin pals. Because first and foremost, the job of every revolution is to survive, like a child. That survival depends on its moronic ability to deny the needs and feelings of everything around it for its own daily sustenance – like a baby screaming to nurse. Whatever else he may have been, Robespierre was a straight arrow, a trajectory unchangeable.

Incorruptible's second definition is to be immune to decay and death. For a mere mortal, this is trickier, though not impossible.

When Robespierre is taken to the guillotine, a giant, blood-stained bandage holds his jaw to his head. The last day he's been in agony, physically and emotionally, so much to say but unable to speak. As he is prepared for the razor, his executioner callously rips off his bandage, probably to ensure it does not interfere with a smooth and certain severing of his head.

Robespierre lets out a horrible, animal-like scream that jolts the assembled crowd. Perhaps it's all those words trapped in his chest, or just the very real pain of being mortal, proving his fragile humanity, or just the infantile scream of needing to nurse, desperate to keep his revolutionary baby alive just one day more. Whatever it means, it will be the last noise he makes as he is placed on the plank, brought horizontal, locked into a lunette like the ones to which he sent so many. He must be so tired at this point, and his head is brought to rest.

He dies. We will never see him again.

W*e* *find* *ourselves* alone at the Musée de la Révolution Française at Vizille. It's a weekday, and Vizille isn't exactly Paris, so it's quiet. No one is here, not even any security guards, as we rapidly move through the galleries. We're not patient people, so we don't slow down much and rarely read placards. We're busy thinking about the hot chocolate and croissants that must be waiting for us when we are done with this. We pass beneath chandeliers and distractedly admire suits of armor, but mostly, we just enjoy this regal palace that contains the revolutionary museum. It is such a tasteful piece of irony.

Like most museums, it teems with props and mixed messages. Porcelain busts (and I mean, literally, bare busts) of women declaring liberty and equality sit illuminated by the elaborate chandeliers of some long-gone royal. You can take in a chipped marble plaque about the radical Marat or lose yourself in a painting of the guillotine while sitting on a luxurious couch in a room fit for a king.

It is just the kind of synthesis the French are so adept at, their pride in their history fusing with forward-thinking ideals, all in place of sensual splendor. In a sense, it's what all museums do: flatten the violence of the past by venerating all of it. You may not have survived the reign of terror, but your palace did as did a bunch of other objects. The war is over – let's revel in our Frenchness.

So, all is well. We move through the galleries. We turn a corner.

And suddenly, there he is in the middle of the room. We had the sneaking suspicion we might bump into him, and here he is. How very awkward for us, especially after badmouthing him for the last few dozen pages.

He is formed of red clay like a golem, shaped into a terracotta bust, seemingly inanimate, not likely to talk back. This makes him approachable. So, we do, finding him additionally encased in a glass box and sliced at the shoulders, a near approximation of the truth. Surprisingly, he looks reasonable, even friendly. We read on the placard that this bust was made by the deaf and mute sculptor Claude-André Deseine, and we wonder if this is why it is such a sympathetic capture. Being able to tune out Robespierre's torrent of words might have given him special insight. Or, put another way, he never had to actually listen to the revolutionary bloviate.

Robespierre is glancing off to the side, one shoulder down, sending him in motion, and that sets us in motion, too. Stepping around the bust, we try to find level ground, a steady place to engage him. It is so quiet in the room, we are so alone and so focused, that it feels like surgery. We get above the vitrine, looking down, and see his compassionate, hopeful spirit.

We outflank him, moving left, and feel his confidence. He's somebody we would follow, trustworthy and dependable. Then, we move around to his right and are reminded of his rigidity and arrogance. We disdain his disdain.

We crouch down into a squat to see him from below, and he looks fearful. Bad sign. We can't stay here too long – our knees aren't strong nor is Robespierre's tolerance for discomfort. Too often his feeling of fear translates to the end of feelings altogether for others.

Restlessly, we move around the bust to find a Maximilien we can live with, maybe even appreciate, but we are all too aware that there is a Maximilien we cannot survive only a few inches to our left or right, above or below. It is, as the French like to say, absurd. We inch around a glass box in an empty room in a palace dedicated to the end of palaces, trying to get comfortable.

For all our pains and maneuvering, the bust stays the same. Robespierre never changes. We exist in tranquility provided by time, but we are anxious, moving around a fixed piece of red earth, hunting for a safe place to stay, to lay our head down, and come to rest.

An ox drawn cart with a printing press, a 2400 member chorus, a 40 foot tall plaster mountain – welcome, my friends, to the Festival of the Supreme Being: a one day, all-you-can-eat, bat-crap-crazy reprieve from the guillotine. Two days later the law of 22 Prarial will be passed – the Great Terror has begun!!! What happened on 21 Prairial?

A surprisingly compassionate rendering of Maxmillien Robbespierre by the Sculptor Claude-André Deseine. It might have helped that Deseine was a deaf mute and never had to listen to Robespierre give a speech.

7
CHALK
9 APRIL | 27 MARCH 1917

But do you know who made Maximilien Robespierre look like a mild-mannered barrel of laughs? Владимир Ульянов, that's who. You probably know him as Владимир Ленин or just Ленин.

He is often confused with Джон Леннон when brought up in casual conversation, bringing to mind lyrics like, "*Представь, что все люди Живут в мире.*" But that is not the Ленин I'm talking about, and this one isn't all that concerned with мире and is actually likely to spit on the ground if anyone even brings up the prospect of мире. This Ленин doesn't like to sit around воображая things. He prefers Маркс and would rather bring the next and final historical stage into reality. This Ленин isn't a famous singer; though, he did end up on just as many posters as the other Леннон, if not more.

Oh, I'm sorry, it just occurred to me that you might not

have taken four years of Russian in high school like I did. In that case, the Cyrillic alphabet might be a lot to tackle, taking into account the brevity of this book. As a straight D student, and the bane of Mr. Hall's existence, I still pride myself in being able to say, "Yes" and, "What?" and, "Good" and, "Goodbye." Though, for some reason, I can't remember how to say "Hello." It's one of the hardest languages in the world to learn, but you might not know that as you did not take it for four years in high school despite having clearly struggled with the material. Talk about resilience.

I'm actually writing about Lenin, Vladimir Lenin, who I must admit is a pretty resilient guy himself. And wildly disagreeable. In fact, aside from being the originator of a century of Marxist suffering, his most notable achievement is that he was simultaneously a vitriolic pain in the ass while attracting a dedicated following of pretty women and wealthy boot lickers to fund his whimsy.

To be sure, times have changed. Whereas now the ability to recreate 30-second viral booty-shaking dances might get you invited to state dinners, back in the early 20th century, you might get there by sitting in cafes, writing tracts on the means of production, and laying into your rivals as if you were slaughtering a wild hog.

Lenin is good at both, writing page-turners like *Imperialism, the Highest Stage of Capitalism*, while denouncing other Marxists as vermin or detestable centrists or demanding that the worker's movement be purged of, "filth which has accumulated during the score of peaceful years." So yeah, Джон

Леннон, he's not into peace, but he might be cool with the "no possessions" part.

Right now, he is on a cramped train moving through Germany with the goal of killing the Tsar and pushing Russia into a revolution that will resolve the course of human history. This is his long-term ambition, anyway.

Presently, he is more concerned by the cigarette smoke coming from the toilet stall. Smoking is not part of achieving a classless and stateless society. It's just another capitalist ploy to mollify the masses. Plus, he can't stand smoke, so he has forbidden it from the train car outside of the toilet stall. But now, he can't help but notice smokers are dominating the stall to get their nicotine fix. Other people in line might legitimately be looking to do a #1, or even working on a #2, and as you know, anyone working is given priority in a Marxist world. So, he is compelled to create a new order around the use of the toilet with tickets for people defecating and tickets for people smoking. Crappers – the workers – get priority, of course.

Lenin is surrounded by fellow socialists, so-called comrades, but he can't stomach the smoke, and so this new system, and justification, is invented. He's also sick of people on the train singing the Marseillaise. While I can totally relate, it is petty to deny these party people on the eve of their great victory. But Lenin – who is, let's be honest, a born petty tyrant – needs conditions to be just right in order to achieve his aims.

And there is never any doubt who the most important

person is on this train because that person is a born petty tyrant. And if this train is going to bring about a historical change, and maybe even the perfect society, perhaps a little petty tyranny is justified. Thus, it logically follows that power must consolidate to one individual for the whole to survive.

So, is this where the birth of Lenin's dictatorship of the proletariat is born? On a smoky train hurtling through Germany? The answer to that is, surprisingly, yes. Definitely *yes*. Because one of the reasons Lenin behaves so disagreeably, longing for silence and clean air, is that he is furiously scribbling his famous – or rather infamous – *April Theses*, an act of revisionism that makes Luther's 95 theses look like a Post-it note by comparison. Lenin, in his mounting megalomania and euphoria as he steams toward Russia, overturns fundamental Marxist truths, stating that a bourgeoisie capitalist stage is unnecessary for achieving a socialist revolution and arguing that democracy is untenable in the face of the resistance presented by capitalist elements. There must be a coalescing of power in one person who can shepherd the interests of the proletariat into a successful revolution. And guess who that might be?

Quite frankly, the claustrophobic rattling down the track of this sealed train can easily serve as a road map for a number of problems of the future Soviet state. Maybe the smoke exacerbated Lenin's severe atherosclerosis, which would kill him in 1924 and leave a power vacuum to be filled by товарищ Сталин.

Perhaps, before his death, Lenin told Stalin about his

issues with the smoke and the system he created on the train to manage it, and this process of identification and stigmatizing inspired Stalin to conduct his purges. Are these long lines to the toilet foreshadowing the long lines that will show up 60 years later on the streets of Moscow, comrades queuing up for toilet paper?

But we might be looking too closely into the toilet on the train, and it is not, generally speaking, a good idea to look too closely into the toilet on a train. In fact, there are some people on board, especially this cranky fella Lenin, who would rather we pretend this train did not exist. Forget the train, forget who is on it, forget what country it is moving through. Pretend we see nothing.

But try as we might, nagging questions remain. Cigarette smoke and off-tune renditions of the Marseillaise are minor issues. More interesting, potentially embarrassing, probably problematic, and definitely awkward is the train itself – and not just the train car, but the tracks it is running on, and the land on which those tracks are built, not to mention the checkpoints and customs stations and national boundaries that are being cut through like warm butter.

It is hard not to wonder who is paying for all this, who is helping to make such an unlikely journey go so smoothly. The Vladimir Lenin of 1917 is barely in a position to buy a ticket to the zoo, much less afford an entire party car for a couple of dozen of his most cherished sycophants. And even if he did have the money, he did not possess the geopolitical clout to cut through national borders on his way back to St.

Petersburg. He is a Russian Marxist traveling through the mother of all right-wing countries: Germany – a place that will shortly give birth to Nazism – a party that will prioritize the eradication of Marxists like Lenin.

But the strangest thing of all is on the floor of the train. It is a chalk line with two chalk arrows, one pointing to the front of the train and designating it as Russian, the other pointing to the back half, designating it as German. In and of itself, this might seem like a harmless joke. Or perhaps a small child of one of these Marxists got loose with a piece of chalk, and being the toddler of a Marxist, doodling a Marxist toddler's musing (try saying that five times fast).

But looking up now, we see it's actually true. At the back of the train, it's all Germans, soldiers sitting quietly and sullenly, waiting for this trip to end, whereas in the front it's mostly Russians, all cheerful and singing and smoking in the bathroom. And while we can't get outside to see the doors of the train right now, since it is moving, if we could we would see chalk writing on the door saying "SEALED." Discreetly, we asked around about this, and apparently, Lenin had his Swiss pal Fritz Platten do the chalk markations. Even though it's chalk, the softest rock you can find on Planet Earth, everyone is taking it totally seriously like it really means something. The chalk is telling us that, at this point, in spite of reality, the front of the train is not a train at all but a small piece of Russia crossing Germany.

So, obviously, now we're really curious. We could have stomached the cigarette smoke and the issue about the money, but the chalk is too much. Sure, Lenin doesn't want us asking any questions, and we're scared of him, but there comes a point when you can no longer live in darkness. Lenin can get as cranky as he wants and focus on the foibles and shortcomings of his best friends, but we are not one of his starry-eyed underlings and we want some answers.

Just what the hell is going on here?

TWO YEARS EARLIER, we were on a bus. There are three other buses in our caravan, lumbering down bumpy roads heading to a tiny village in Switzerland called Zimmerwald for a conference. Supposedly, it's an ornithologists' conference. You know, bird watching. But as these four buses disgorge their passengers in front of the Hotel Beau Séjour, there's a suspicious lack of binoculars or field guides. Like bird watchers, they are a high-strung set, cranky introverts who crave company if only to have someone to abuse; but they do not have that nature-loving vibe. Bimaculated larks and blacktailed godwits fly all over the place, and no one in the group seems to notice or care, which again prompts the question we asked a minute ago. What the hell is going on here?

It's quite an international group. Swiss, Italians, Germans, an assortment of weirdo Balkan types, as well as some Russians. There's a decidedly shabby quality to this subspecies of human beings as if they're all roommates in a dilapidated mansion who outfitted themselves in the same Transylvanian thrift store – birds of a weathered feather flocking together. But they are serious and walk with purpose, especially this one guy with a neck like a bull and small, piercing eyes. His walk is more of a stride as if he is determined to get somewhere, even if that means just getting up and going for a cup of coffee.

That's Lenin. Vladimir Lenin. Or, as you now know him, Владимир Ленин.

Lenin is definitely no bird watcher. This fabricated excuse for the conference is an attempt to elude a secret police presence. But it is an entirely unnecessary evasion because guess what? It is 1915, and Europe is at war. Maybe a couple of years back fears of an imminent Communist revolution would have prompted secret police to come up with their own implausible reason to sleep at the Hotel Beau Séjour and spy, but now the vogue of socialism is yesterday's news. War is the red-hot trend. No one gives a damn about a bunch of unshowered socialists gathering in the middle of nowhere to not look at birds.

Perhaps Comrade Trotsky, hipster extraordinaire, says it best as he leaves his bus, and beholding the scene, says, "Half a century after the formation of the First International, it is still possible to fit all European internationalists into four coaches."

Does Lenin hear his comment? For Trotsky's sake, I hope not. Lenin lacks a sense of humor. Besides, as a Hegelian, a Marxist, and an adherent to the insignificance of man in the face of history, he wouldn't put much store in counting heads. Let us not forget, "the Wittenberg Convergence," the now-famous addition to the *Stanford Encyclopedia of Philosophy*. As we know, abject obscurity is sometimes the best launch pad, and a small handful of delusional, humorless people really can change history.

At least if they're humorless, delusional people like Lenin. For 30 years, he has been harassed, arrested, imprisoned, and exiled. He's founded the Bolshevik Party, a name which literally means the "majority party," even though they are decidedly not. He has backed bank robbers to deal with insufficient funds. He has squabbled with fellow socialists, spewing forth torrents of vitriol and rage on people who share his goal while scarcely mentioning the shortcomings of the Tsar. He has been on the run for years, first in Paris, which he detests, then in London, which he detests even more, and now in Switzerland, which he actually kind of likes but feels obliged to pretend to detest.

He and his wife and his mistress bump around Europe like three blind mice, landing in crappy flats, eating bad food, and frequently getting sick. Lenin works himself into a froth daily, furiously scribbling so much it's a wonder he doesn't contract carpal tunnel syndrome, hardening his personality even more and becoming a bastard in the process.

Wow, hold on. Does this sound like anyone else we know?

Well, as it should happen, Lenin is a big fan of Robespierre. Years later, he will even erect a statue of him; however, due to poor materials and shoddy engineering, it falls into rubble in a few days, which kind of sounds like the

Soviet Union. Though, that collapse will take considerably longer. Sadly.

Like Robespierre, Lenin has become practiced in the art of maintaining a clear position. The best way to maintain a clear position, alas, is to be extreme. Whereas Maximilien had a few moderating tendencies, however slight, Lenin eliminates all daylight between him and the furthest-left position. Because nothing can come of a blended position that incorporates nuance and shades of gray when you want to overthrow a Tsar. Lenin is a child of Marx, and his goal is simple: revolution. What comes next, comes next.

But being extreme is a lonely life, and it might make you appear to be a delusional loser. You may even *be* a delusional loser. Because, while we all know the name Lenin, history is littered with insufferable pedants who followed similar paths but never amounted to squat. History is the study of winners, even if they are losers. That is to say, the mere fact that we're studying them signifies their status as winners of a kind. So, it is easy to find someone like us to keep our hopes alive, but most of us, alas, will not be studied. It's not so bad if you have a sense of humor and remind yourself that graveyards are filled with important people, and besides, one day the sun will expand and engulf the earth in its entirety. Isn't that heartening?

Right now, four buses have coughed 38 revolutionaries onto the steps of the sleepy hotel in the sleepy Swiss village. Our ornithologists enter the Hotel Beau Séjour, check in, stow their bags in their room, and proceed to the big meeting room on the first floor where they close the door and then draw the drapes, which is a very unusual move for a group supposedly dedicated to watching birds.

In fact, most will barely venture outside in the next few days; though Lenin does, playing with the owner's dogs, perhaps because he's so dogmatic. (Rimshot!) There are other times when, annoyed with other socialists at the conference, he just storms out of the Hotel Beau Séjour in a fury, probably because he is so problematic.

And why is he angry? Because, like Джон Леннон, all some of the other delegates *are saying....is to give peace a chance.*

Peace? Lenin is disgusted. Peace does not produce historical progress; besides, the war is the perfect time to press the issue. Lenin seeks civil war and revolution, looking to harness the fatigue and rage on all sides. Right-wing socialists (I know, an oxymoron of a kind, but they exist) at the conference call for an end to the war and are, to Lenin's mind, alarmingly hung up on nationalist issues like Germany respecting Belgium's neutrality.

For the love of God, have they not read Marx? Don't they know this is the International, a movement seeking to eliminate the borders put in place by greedy imperialists? If Lenin had any of his once-red hair left, he'd be pulling it out by now. Instead, he just storms in and out of the hotel, dogmatically plays with the owner's dogs, goes for brooding walks in the shadow of the Alps, and curses the delegates back in the conference room.

In all fairness, he has a point. The war is not even a year old and already people are disappointed by it. It wasn't even supposed to last a year, and now all the soldiers on the Western Front are running around in the bowels of the Earth getting either bombed, shot, or their nerves stripped bare. The Eastern Front isn't much better – cold, open, and dangerously flat. Here, we have a war so very clearly being fought for capitalism and imperialism between first cousins intent on enslaving the masses, and some delegates at Zimmerwald are worried about Belgium-this and Germany-that. They're cowards. They've lost their nerve. Only Lenin, and a few close zealots, can see it clearly, forming the Zimmerwald Left and calling for a Third International, whatever the hell that means.

A few days of this storming and dogmatism and the conference comes to a close. A manifesto is completed, and Lenin emerges as the loser. It's barely a manifesto at all, does not have the strident tone so important to any endeavor, and just wants to give peace a chance, as if the powers to be are even interested in that.

Everyone packs their bags, having by now probably entirely forgotten the cover of having been at a bird-watching conference. As they line up to leave in the driveway, perhaps this time Trotsky thinks twice about cracking the joke about the socialist movement fitting into four buses.

Because disagreements have been rife in the prior days, wounds need to be licked, and if they're not careful, the socialist movement of Europe might soon be reduced to fitting on a tandem bike.

There's not a train in sight.

BUT THERE ARE TRENCHES. Lots and lots of trenches. Nearly everyone had thought the war would be a necessary house cleaning, a quick six-month affair. Now, it has turned into a surprisingly unpleasant meat grinder. Armies sink into the ground, digging their own graves. It is less a match of strategy and more a question of logistics. Combatant nations feed shells, boots, bullets, and most importantly, people to the front line like a string of numbers disappearing into a shredder. Something has to give. The stranglehold must be broken. The most logical way to break out of a deadlock like this is to either open up a new front or close down an existing one.

The British try the former, attempting to seize the Turkish Straits from the Ottomans. From there, they figure they can work their way up the Balkans to harass the Austro-Hungarians. This will draw resources from the Western Front, a new wound will be opened, and the Central Powers will bleed to death. Plus, the straits will be open to resupply Russia and receive stockpiled grain in return. It's a win-win, but only if you win-win it, and they don't. It actually ends up a lose-lose, with the British Navy crapping its britches in the face of the Dardanelles, and the British army sacrificing thousands in a vain attempt to mount Gallipoli. They do get painfully close to achieving their aims, and a few decisions might have changed history, but it is not to be, and no new front appears in the Great War.

The Germans, on the other hand, dream of closing down a front. Seeing that the Western one is seemingly impervious to change, the Eastern Front becomes the object of their designs. Russia is fundamentally weak, at least in terms of munitions and provisions production. The Turkish Straits remain closed, which means the underequipped Russians can't be easily resupplied by their allies. Besides this, they are a backward nation and do not have their hands on the latest weapons. All they have going for them are lots and lots of people they can push into the line of machine gun fire. And the more those people are mowed down, the angrier the people around them and the relatives back home become.

The last time Russia did poorly in a war, in 1905 against the Japanese, they nearly had a revolution. Now, the Germans have them on the ropes. The Russians are wheezing and spitting out teeth, but then again, the Russians are nothing if not willing to take a massive amount of punishment. They've been trained by centuries of Tsars and perennial merciless weather to keep their mouths shut unless they're downing a shot of vodka.

Britain knows perfectly well about Russia's weakness and is determined to keep them in the war. It is one of the reasons the British attempted to take the Turkish Straits in the first place, laying possession of them, so they could dangle them in front of Russia, keeping them fighting. When that fails, they go hypothetical and stuff two midlevel diplomats, Mark

Sykes and Francois George Picot, in a room to carve up maps of the Ottoman Empire for their eventual consumption, now dangling the theoretical prospect of giving the Straits to Russia as motivation.

But Russia remains strangely unmoved. Almost catatonic. It's just so vast and cold and stoic and suffering that, quite frankly, it's hard to move. But as Sykes and Picot carve up the Middle East, ruining it for a century and more, their promise of the Turkish Straits to Russia barely gets a nod. It's as if Russia is past the point of caring, so inwardly corrupt and checked-out and fatalistic that they know what's coming next, dread it, and can consider little else.

Russians are being chewed up at the front by the thousands, shortages abound everywhere, and the normally docile natives are getting restless. The Tsar and his wife are being (poorly) advised by a greasy-haired mystic while the nobles of St. Petersburg party like it's 1348. Meanwhile, the factory workers and peasant stock have basically had enough. They don't know it yet, but the former's hammer is about to cross with the latter's sickle.

It sure will make a great flag.

So, if you're Germany, facing internal dissent and widespread strikes yourself, it makes sense to poke Russia into a full-blown revolution that will remove it from the war and collapse the Eastern Front. The Tsar is catatonic; his resources are dwindling fast. If the Germans can remove him, they have a fighting chance to win this thing.

If only they could get a helping hand.

. . .

Meet Israel Lazarevich Helphand. If you like, you can call him by his Marxist nickname, Parvus. Outside of getting to wear lots of red and correcting all the world's ills, another cool thing about being a Marxist is that you can take one-word names like you're a superhero – like Stalin, Man of Steel, no relation to Clark Kent, Man of Steel, or Clark's predecessor, Doc Savage, also Man of Steel.

Were I a Marxist myself, my moniker would be весельчак, but you'll have to Google translate that one in your free time. The point is, it's cool to be a socialist back then, kind of like being a well-read vampire, and Parvus just may be both, and a few other things to boot, like an international arms dealer, geopolitical fixer, and trusted advisor to the untrustworthy Young Turks of the Sublime Porte.

"Parvus" means small in Latin, and this is just another one of his many contradictions because small Parvus is not. He is a mountain of flesh, bulging in all directions and sleek like a duck so fat that it cannot fly. His small, duck-like legs barely hold his heft, eyes protruding out of a bald head. In fact, a duck is a good metaphor for a man so slippery and amphibious, one who can waddle on the *terra firma* of the Marxist International or bob in the choppy waters of capitalist ports.

Let's start with the waddle. Like Lenin, Parvus is radicalized in his teens and gets busy building his Marxist CV. He is part of the 1905 uprising in Russia, chumming it up with

Trotsky and promoting the concept of "Permanent Revolution," which calls for killing rich people in perpetuity. I'm not sure how an idea like that qualifies as a theory, but it is refreshingly direct, even if it does presume a limitless supply of rich people.

It is also ironic because as Parvus is being sent into Siberian exile he escapes and lands in Istanbul where he wades into some shady business. He gets rich trading war goods to an ailing Ottoman Empire, exchanging his moth-eaten Marxist coat for a wardrobe of snappy tuxedos. It really is quite a feat; he has gone from promoting a theory of permanent revolution to becoming the object of its scorn. According to his own logic, he's now one of the rich people who needs to be killed all the time.

He performs this transformation cheerfully, shamelessly, and not the least fearfully, perhaps because he knows the effectiveness of revolutionary socialists firsthand. These socialists are more inclined to blow one another up than the Tsar, so he's not sweating an impending revolution. He is more likely to be killed by the champagne and sausage he consumes for breakfast or by one of his many mistresses. He's having the time of his life, and it may cost him his life.

If all of this sounds bizarre to you, get in line. Parvus is what one blogger called, "an antisemitic fever dream." Though, he is less an all-knowing cabal leader as he is adept at riding chaos for personal gain, an overweight, opportunistic surfer catching political waves crashing along European shores.

In fact, if you're looking for a master puppeteer you would do better looking at Parvus' mentor, Basil Zaharoff, a Greek – and Christian – merchant of death. Basil's fingers are in every stewing pot on the continent. He manages, at age 74, to marry the beautiful María del Pilar Antonia Angela Patrocinio Fermina Simona de Muguiro y Beruete, 1st Duchess de Villafranca de los Caballeros, who is already one of the richest people in Spain even before she marries Basil.

Compared to Zaharoff, Parvus is a junior account manager in the global domination racket and will never reach Basil's exalted levels of corruption and excess. But Parvus does have high friends in low places and low friends in high places. For example, there's rumors he's in pay of the British; though, he'll double-cross them later.

Parvus sees an opportunity to profit from his past socialist activities because now he's on the team where the downfall of the Tsar and the destruction of Russia are hot talking points. And, as it should happen, he knows a circle of people who have been totally working on this very problem for years. In fact, he himself used to be part of their team. Team Marx.

And so, he takes this valuable knowledge to the German embassy and is then summoned to Berlin. He proposes they give him a bunch of Deutschmarks he can shower on these Russian exiles. That way, they can agitate for a revolution back home in Russia. Do the Germans kick him out of the embassy for requesting money for what is clearly a fool's errand? No, they actually do give him a sack of money and wish him luck.

Because this is 1915, folks. Everyone is everyone else's business. Germans covertly fund newspapers in France. The British make under-the-table payoffs to anyone willing to betray their own country. Russian secret police scurry around Paris, scribbling notes about the people in cafes who are scribbling notes about Russia. The Tsarina listens to pro-German debutantes when she's not consulting her mad monk, Rasputin. Shell companies are set up, smuggling thrives, and propaganda is purchased wholesale. Seen this way, Europe leading up to the First World War is not so much at odds as it is entirely too enmeshed. Decades of peace and burgeoning commerce have made it unclear where all these national lines stop and start. All of this sounds eerily familiar; it can be argued that we are living in a similar world where the elites own apartments in every global city and no election goes unmolested.

As for Parvus, I cannot help but admire a person who monetizes their socialist credentials. He sets off on a tour of Europe, flush with German money, easily able to afford his sausage and champagne regimen. He calls on his old pal Rosa Luxemburg. For some reason – who knows why – she thinks he might be a total fraud. Maybe it's the tuxedos, the diamond rings on his sausage-like fingers, or the fact that he has come around peddling the agenda of an imperialist war machine like Germany. She violently kicks him out of her apartment.

He then approaches Lenin in a restaurant in Berne, and Vlad is put off by being approached publicly, making a big show of rejecting the man. However, he later discreetly meets Parvus in his apartment to hear him out. Like Luxemburg, he doesn't like what he hears and clearly knows Parvus is a scoundrel, but he does not burn his bridges with him. He can plausibly contend that he's rejected Parvus, but he keeps the door open. Because the revolution is coming. He's not sure when, but it is coming. And when the revolution comes, Lenin will need all the friends he can get, even if they are obese arms dealers working for the Kaiser and have bags of money.

Beggars can't be choosers.

EVEN THOUGH HE knows it's coming, Lenin is surprised when the revolution actually arrives. In fact, it surprises just about everyone, which is kind of surprising in itself considering the abject conditions in Russia and the incessant forecast for snow and rebellion. It's triggered by a lack of flour, frozen toilet pipes, and a slight warming trend in February leading to an unusually well-attended women's march. It reads like a Slavic reboot of the French Revolution, but at the time, few thought these factors would be enough to topple a Tsar who still can unleash the military on his own people. Lenin's Bolsheviks in Petrograd sniff at the marchers as they march past, pitying them for their ignorance about proper conditions to launch a revolution.

Huge crowds form, marching across frozen rivers and into the center of the city. But huge crowds of people holding nothing in their hands can just be an opportunity for huge casualties. At one point, lines of Cossack horsemen begin to canter toward the marchers, the steel of their sabers glinting, whips in their free hands. But then, unexpectedly, they slow upon their approach, moving through the crowd like ghosts, inflicting no damage. Another shocker comes the next day from barracks outside the city. Regiments go rogue, staging a mutiny, with younger officers executing older ones. Now, there is nothing to stop the workers, peasants, and enlightened ones from rising. The revolution has begun.

Knowing Lenin as we know him, you can only imagine how hyper this news makes him. For years, he has been a panther in exile, pacing back and forth in his theoretical cage, awaiting the revolution. Now, the revolution has come, and he is behind bars of his own making, stuck in his safe Swiss exile. It's been a great place to hide out, watch birds, nurture grievances, and dream big, but now that change is happening without him. Lenin finds himself inconveniently distant, a few nations away from his homeland, from his moment, from the Revolution.

Desperately, he looks for a way back. One route would take him through England, a Russian ally. But Lenin figures the British likely have him on a blacklist, and he's probably right, so he agitates for a fake passport, figuring he can always wear a wig. This is a passport photo I would pay to see, but the plan goes nowhere, mostly due to Lenin's mistress who is slow to assist. According to Catherine Merridale's excellent *Lenin on a Train*, there's even a scheme to use a Swede's passport and for Lenin to pretend on the sleeper train that he is a mute; a plan that is eliminated once Lenin's wife reminds him that it will never work because Lenin has a tendency to shout invectives in his sleep, in Russian, of course.

There's only one other way to get to Russia.

MEANWHILE, somewhere in Copenhagen, our friend Parvus is having the time of his life. He has parlayed his German connections into a regular cottage industry. Check this out: he's a Russian Marxist turned capitalist moving German goods through Denmark and Sweden into Russia with the help of a Lithuanian-Polish exile, also a lapsed Marxist turned capitalist. All of this gives new meaning to the International. They're repackaging German goods in Denmark to sneak them back into Russian markets, including useful things like condoms and thermometers, hopefully not being used at the same time. As Germany grinds out a war with Russia on a cold and barren front, Parvus gets rich ensuring German manufacturers keep making money and Russians with high temperatures can enjoy sex without the fear of procreation. Pretty meta.

More meta still, Parvus has his German handlers totally sandbagged. Astoundingly, they report back to Berlin that Mr. Champagne & Cigar & Diamond Cufflinks is thriftily handling his budget and is on the cusp of uniting all the different factions of the Russian Revolutionaries. The latter claim, to anyone who knows anything, is laughably implausible. God himself could not do that, especially as we're talking about a pack of committed atheists. The naivety of the Germans is astounding, though it is easy to imagine Parvus paying off anyone sent to monitor him, and that his true genius rests on a strategy of well-placed, well-timed kickbacks.

And then, suddenly, Parvus becomes useful. Exceedingly useful. Through a proxy, he reopens talks with Lenin. The last time they were in communication, Lenin publicly tossed Parvus out on his sizable ass. Now, it's different. Time is of the essence, and there is no alternative but to return to Russia. Through contacts with the German high command, Parvus can get Lenin through Germany. From there, it's a hop, jump, and skip through some neutral powers to St. Petersburg, putting the revolution on a platter for Lenin to consume. Yes, moving through Imperialist Germany through the generosity of a Mad Kaiser strains credibility, and there will be a lot of explaining to do later. Plus, Lenin will have to hold his nose on his way through Deutschland. But surely it beats bird watching in Switzerland as this one and only historical moment passes him by.

Lenin is astute enough to know that Parvus lurks behind the scenes. And being a ball buster of the first order, he begins issuing demands that need to be met if he is to accept the German largesse. For one, the Germans will not be allowed to know the names of the passengers who board the train. This may sound like a small demand. It is not. Anyone could be on this train, including enemies of the Kaiser, getting a free pass through Germany. Very awkward. It almost brings the negotiations to a full stop but not quite. Lenin gets his way.

Lenin's other demand is that the train be granted extraterritorial rights.

Now, this is worth taking a moment to understand and appreciate. Only an ideologue seeped in Marxism and Hegelian dialectics could come up with such a wild condition. In essence, the train car they will occupy will not actually be moving through Germany because it will technically be a part of Russia – a moving part of Russia – clanking down the tracks of the German Fatherland.

In truth, it will only be part of the train car because this mobile piece of the Motherland will not include the German soldiers aboard the train who are put there to watch them. These German soldiers can only do that – watch them – because they will not be able to speak with them or cross over into the section of the train that is Russian territory. Once Lenin and his ragtag army enter this train at the German border, there will be no getting off. This is the "sealed" aspect of the train, which actually will have windows, with starving Germans approaching the car in stations and looking menacingly at the plump Marxists within, well-fed on the bread and cheese of neutral Switzerland. These gaunt characters are beyond the proletariat.

Later, Churchill will call the train the "most grisly of all weapons" and say of Lenin that he was in the sealed car "like a plague bacillus." It's a vivid turn of phrase, though a more impartial view would be to see the sealed train like a gelatin-protected pill. The extraterritorial coating of this pill gets them through the mouth of Germany, growing thin in the trachea of Scandinavian countries, and then the contents of the pill – the medicine, or poison, depending on your position – will be released into the belly of Russia after having passed through the esophagus of St. Petersburg. I could go on and talk about the particulars of the digestive tract and the resulting exit of the excrement, but I'll let you fill in that part with your imagination.

THERE ARE a number of last-minute negotiations. Lenin stubbornly insists that he and his team pay for their own journey across Germany, which will be great for the plausible deniability they'll need later. There's only one problem with that. They're basically broke. Because they're Marxists and not the Parvus kind of Marxist who gets rich selling weapons. So, a collection has to be taken to pay for the tickets. Lenin also insists that his crew be able to bring its own food to sustain them through the sealed passage through Germany. The Germans will agree to this one, but in an ironic twist, neutral Switzerland will confiscate the food on their way out because exporting food is banned during wartime. Duh!

A kind of flash mob shows up at Lenin's departure in Zurich, which will be a normal train ride to the German border. As Lenin's crew moves toward the train station they are booed and hissed at. Insults reign down. Partly, this comes from people who want to be on the train and have not been invited. Partly, it comes from those deriding Lenin for accepting a ride from the Kaiser, the worst kind of Imperialist scum. Irish author, Zurich resident, and aspiring blind man James Joyce may even be in the crowd, marveling at the desperation of the Germans that drives them to sponsor such a farce. Indeed, the scene is strongly reminiscent of a stream of consciousness in its absurdity.

At the German border, the group's food is confiscated, and they're inspected by a pair of shiny-booted, unsmiling proto-Nazis. But at last, they board the train. With them is Fritz Platten, a socialist who happens to be Swiss, so he can act as a neutral party, laying the chalk down the middle of the train to separate the German and Russian nations, as well as writing "SEALED" in chalk on the train doors. Lenin's abstraction is now complete. They are not a bunch of poor radicals on a rattling train, they are an idea floating through time and space, hurtling toward Russia. Only Platten, the neutral, can move between the two countries as the two countries prepare to move down the train tracks. Only Platten can pass forward the sandwiches procured by Germans in the back to Russian Revolutionaries in the front.

And now, with the chalk in place, the train can at last lunge forward. Lenin is free to get upset as cigarettes are lit. He can put his dictatorship of the proletariat in place to rule over the bathroom stall and dream big about what is next. It's possible to dream because Lenin, our dictator, has set strict sleep hours. They are essential if we're going to be well-rested for the revolution, for what comes next. Lenin furiously scribbles away at his *April Theses*, but finally, he falls asleep. After a life of exile, he's earned it. Now, he can dream big.

WE BEGAN this chapter on a train with Lenin, wondering just what the hell was going on. Now, a couple of dozen pages later, we know. Kind of. Sort of. And it still seems almost impossible. A fat Marxist arms dealer gets the Kaiser's government to port an obscure exile across their country so that he can return to Russia and take down the Tsar, removing Russia from the war. What a joke! It's a total moonshot! But guess what? Just like the original moonshot, it works!

Neil Armstrong steps on moon dust talking about one small step for man; Lenin steps down on the platform of Finland Station, declaring, "The people need peace; the people need bread; the people need land. And they give you war, hunger, no bread..." These are words that could have been written by the Kaiser's general staff, leaflets dropped down from planes to demoralize Russia's fighting spirit. For Lenin, with the Germans watching closely, it will be just the beginning of his campaign. He'll spend months taking increasingly extreme positions, roundly mocked by many until he unexpectedly wins the power struggle, and as promised, he removes Russia from the war. Snap. Just like that.

Imagine the laughter and glee in the rooms of the Kaiser's

staff. All they did was give him a ride across Germany and look the other way. Now the Tsar is done, the Eastern Front is closed. Not a bad return on their investment.

But they won't be laughing long. Russia's move toward radical socialism is one of the key causes for America entering the war and joining the Western Front. Germany, already wheezing, will soon be exhausted from all these years of fighting. Strikes and revolts break out all over the country. Left-wing agitators gained traction, and now, Germany has a hulking Red Soviet mass to the east to worry about. The Kaiser's staff turns out to be too clever by half, which is common in spy craft. It's amazing what you can pull off, but it's more remarkable what unexpectedly comes next.

The sequel will make all this look rather quaint.

LIKE ROBESPIERRE, Lenin gives me the heebie-jeebies. Actually, even more so because while Robespierre's red bust sits in the Musée de la Révolution Française, Lenin's actual corpse is alive and unwell in Moscow. You can visit him from 10 to 1 every day except Fridays and Mondays. It's free of charge, which is pretty generous of the Russian Federation considering it costs them $200,000 every year to keep the body from disintegrating. Yes, he looks a little like a sweating candle, and no one has seen him move in a while, but I imagine him, in his free time, stepping out of his tricked-out coffin to stretch his legs. Visitors and guards are all gone, and somehow, he accesses the Internet. He comes across this book, maybe even tries to pirate it from a torrent site, and failing that, begrudgingly forks over Russian bitcoinage to download it onto his Kindle.

Reading, he feels some sympathy for Caesar, is cautiously interested in Luther, and is extravagantly dismissive of Washington. No doubt, he gets steaming mad at my portrayal of Robespierre. But that heat is just the warm-up for when he hits the chapter about the chalk. Now, he's really mad, muttering to himself, cursing my name, and fantasizing about tossing me out on my ass. Because that's what Lenin did a lot: he tossed people out on their asses.

But to Lenin, the corpse, who might be reading these very words in an empty mausoleum, I say this: You may not be happy about all this talk about chalk and your sealed train, Влад, but at least I didn't bring up all the German gold. How about that? Want me to do a follow-up chapter called German Gold?

Yeah, I didn't think so.

OF ALL THE objects in this book, the chalk interests me the most. It's been with us always – on cave walls, on chalkboards, on sidewalks, on train cars – from the very first time we held it as a species without opposable thumbs and recounted our hunting glories to groundbreaking equations that warp the future. It is both temporary and timeless, formed 100 million years ago and still in demand, even in our very virtual present. Chalk is freedom. You can create without commitment. If you've drawn a crowd around you, be it as a teacher in a classroom or a toddler with a parent hovering over your shoulder, there's a sense of anticipation about what's next. Anything can be done with chalk. There are no rules.

Because of this, it is lawless. How many teachers over the years had to go for a bucket of soapy water because of something written on the blacktop of a playground? How many secrets have ended up on the walls of abandoned buildings, waiting for the right person to see them before the rain washes them away? Spray paint is a commitment and one whose intoxicating fumes will mark your fidelity. Chalk is a gamble. It is betting on being exposed or forgotten, which depends on the weather and who might see it first. It is simultaneously cowardly and brave.

So, what about Fritz Platten, the Swiss socialist who helped organize the sealed train? He served as the "neutral" go-between for the Russians in the front of the car and the Germans in the back, passing food forward. He was the man with the chalk who wrote the word "sealed" on the train doors and drew a line down the middle designating national territories on the moving carriage. A year later, he'll save Lenin from an assassination attempt, taking a bullet (albeit only a grazing) for his boss. Platten seems brave, but the act of wielding the chalk does not. It seems small, the thinnest excuse to cover the true nature of the train. Besides, Platten was controlled by Lenin. He was given the chalk, told where to apply it, and what to say. So, in this case, he is neither cowardly nor brave, just a lowly proxy. Lame. For all his pains, he will be executed in Stalin's purges 20 years later. Khrushchev will "rehabilitate" him a decade after that, but that's cold comfort for a corpse, especially one that doesn't get round-the-clock care like Lenin's.

And what about Lenin, who won't apply the chalk himself but has the designs for it? There's no way Lenin is a coward, but it's hard to think of him as brave either. He is too distracted, pedantic, and monomaniacal to be counted as courageous. He has an air of historical inevitability and is blind to dangers that might sideline him. But he is at least audacious, which resides in the same neighborhood as bravery. He seeks permanent change, and in the name of centuries of underclass suffering, he is free to behave poorly along the way and impress himself on the world in a way that will lead to 70 years of suffering for the underclass (and the overclass and the middle class and everyone else in Russia, not to mention its many enslaved proxies of the future).

But let's forget about Platten and Lenin for a moment and imagine the fate of the German soldiers who rode in the back of the sealed train, saying nothing. They were given the banal, mystifying, and frankly, insulting job of watching an unwashed pack of Russian socialists move across the fatherland. Here they have been fighting unwashed Russians on the front for years, and now they have to babysit them, endure their repeated choruses of the Marseillaise, and watch the bald guy Lenin browbeat the rest of them about smoking. What a farce!

Later, after they drop off Lenin, he proceeds to Russia and does his damage to the Tsar in that wicked basement, and his name is splashed all over the German newspaper. Do these German soldiers reflect on their strange train trip? Do they recount the conditions, remembering the singing and the smoking and the smell of sausage and sweat? The bald man took Russia out of the war, and still, the Germans lost? How is this possible? And to add insult to injury, now there's a bunch of communists running around Germany threatening revolution.

If it weren't true, no one would believe it.

But let's switch gears for a moment and think about something that isn't true. Let's imagine, for a moment, two of these German soldiers meeting after the war and reminiscing about their time on the sealed train. Let's call them Leopold and Karl and say that they are aimless after the war, vagabonds without familial ties or work or romantic prospects. They run into one another in a train yard in Hamburg, drink cheap gin in front of a fire made of scrap wood, and recall this Lenin character, reminiscing about that strange ride in the back of the train and how there were these chalk markings on the door that said it was sealed, whatever the hell that meant. Stranger still, there were chalk lines on the floor and were these Bolshie bastards crazy or what? Because according to them, one part of the train was in Russia while the other part was still in Germany. Nuts!

But as they talk – and drink – they begin to wonder if they could find that train, and if they could, whether those chalk lines on the floor would be worth something to someone. Because it's a piece of history and people buy all kinds of dumb stuff from history. So, they might even get rich off it. They drink gin and dream big and fall asleep. In the morning, they push through their hangovers and start searching the Hamburg train yard for the car. They both know it's a long shot, but it's something to do and binds them together. (Besides, it's not like either of them has anything important to do.) Karl is almost certain "F" was the call letter and almost sure it was followed by an 8 and a 6. After that, he's less certain. But how many F86(...) train cars can there possibly be in the fleet? They find nothing in Hamburg, so they hop on a train to Berlin, hiding in one of the unused cars.

There they meet a conductor, Otto, who is supposed to kick stowaways off the train, only they get to talking and it turns out Otto was in the war, too – in the navy – mostly in the Turkish Straits. Otto is like them, and they tell him their plan. Otto wants in and can help. He has access to train logs in Berlin and can see what turns up. More importantly, he tells them about this obese character who lives in a mansion in Berlin and goes by the name of Parvus. Apparently, this guy Parvus is the one who set up the sealed train, and he's rich, so if they can find the floor and find Parvus, they'll make the sale for sure.

Why not? Rich people buy all kinds of dumb stuff.

They get to the Berlin Outer Freight Ring by morning.

Otto checks the records; there are a few promising leads, and they begin to search the yard. But it's pretty large, and they're at it for hours with no luck. It's almost night, and they're about to give up when Leopold spots a train car with a ghostly smudge of chalk on the door. It does not have the call letters that Karl recalled, but it does have a sign affixed to the door reading: **Geschlossen auf Anordnung von German Reich Deutsches Reich.** The Weimar Republic has put this train off limits – sealed, so to speak – and that, plus the ghost of chalk, convinces Leopold that they have stumbled upon Lenin's ride. It's promising, but neither Karl nor Otto wants to break the government seal. However, Leopold pays it no mind, and soon, they're in the car. The sunlight is fading now. They can barely see inside, but Leopold has a lighter, and they begin to scan the floor for chalk drawings.

What they find is a disappointment, at least to Otto and Karl. There are indeed chalk lines on the floor, but they're hopelessly smudged. You can barely make out the marking: **ГЕРМАНИЯ** ← → Germanyia. It's just the ghost of it. Otto and Karl consider it a lost cause, and quite frankly, they don't want to get caught in the sealed car, but Leopold takes the lead. He begins searching the car for chalk, saying if they can find the chalk, too, well that'd be worth something. They can rewrite the marking on the floor then yank the boards up and go find Parvus. Nervous about the noise that would make, Karl tells Leopold that they could grab any piece of wood and pass it off as the real thing, but Leopold, searching the car for a piece of chalk, won't hear of it. He tells Karl and Otto that it has to be from this car – that if they're going to have an object to sell it must come from here. Because if you're going to perpetuate a scam, you have to believe in it.

Leopold is now very much in charge. He is not scared of train yard policemen or getting caught. He's too focused on finding the chalk. And Karl and Otto, who just the night before would have protested Leopold taking the reins, submit to him. Leo is in charge because he's in charge. It's the way he's acting as if nothing will go wrong, and his confidence calms them down. Ceding power to Leopold strangely makes them feel more powerful themselves. So, Karl falls in line and has an inspiration. He heads toward the front of the train to the cabin where Lenin was sitting, and sure enough, he emerges holding a piece of chalk.

Now, they are all swept up in the moment with Leopold in the lead. Otto leaves the car on his own as Leopold carefully reapplies the marking to the floor: **ГЕРМАНИЯ** ← → **Germanyia**. And Otto returns with a metal bar with which they can pry the board loose. No one is worried about getting caught now because they have a leader, Leopold, and that makes them more than just three lost veterans wandering a train yard. Now, they're making history.

And they pry the board up off the floor. Leo tells them to look at the hole in the floor and never forget it. He says it's the hole in the floor that makes the board important. The chalk was always there. They never reapplied it. "Believe!" Leo commands the others, "Believe!" Karl and Otto look at the dark hole, at the gravel and train ties beneath, and they are filled with purpose. It's the *geist*, as they call it in these parts. They're no longer a group of losers seeking a small fortune. They're more than that now. All thanks to their leader, Leopold.

They're a movement.

And a movement needs money.

Time to find Parvus.

Left: Vladimir Lenin, clearly overjoyed. Right: Israel Lazarevich Gelfand, A.K.A. Parvus – one of the strangest humans of the 20th Century, a Marxist who brought about revolution while drinking champagne for breakfast in his mansion outside of Berlin.

A glorified version of Lenin's time on the "sealed" train, making him appear to be a man of the people, which he most certainly was not. He hated people. Especially rich is all the smoking, a capitalist activity Lenin immediately outlawed on the train outside of the toilet.

8

UMBRELLA
SEPTEMBER 30, 1938 | NOVEMBER 22, 1963

LET'S PLAY HISTORICAL CHARADES, shall we? We're in the drawing room of my Kensington townhouse in London because where else would you find yourself playing historical charades but a posh spot like this? There's a roaring fire in the ingle, and everyone has a sherry because that's what fashionable people drink when attending a game of historical charades in a Kensington townhouse.

I've actually never tasted sherry before if I'm being honest. Also, I'm not totally sure how I got here in this townhouse, and I haven't even been upstairs to check out my new house, but so far, I like what I see. I'm not even sure what an ingle is. Apparently, the house cost me four million pounds, paid from the advance to write this book, so it better be nice. Outside, it's an absolute soaker, and while I like rain, as a "Yank" I'm not accustomed to just how much of it falls from the sky here. Londoners are always at the ready for it, unsheathing brollies like the noble knights of yore while I find myself too often running through the streets trying to find a place to get dry.

As the host, I'm up first for charades. I've been given an event. Well, it's kind of an event. Actually, it's something between a sentiment and an event. It's also something you might hurl as an accusation. Or you might call it an attitude of sorts. But wait, I'm not playing by the rules. This is charades. I'm supposed to keep my mouth shut, right? Okay, my mouth is shut.

I hold up one finger. The assembled crowd of brilliant and beautiful Londoners responds in unison, "One word!"

Just so, I nod and take a moment to figure out just what I'd like to do next. Dropping down a bit, using my legs as springs, I present to the gathering an invisible object in my outstretched hands, wait for it to register, and then discard it. Now, I look up, squinting, seemingly disturbed, and put my hand up to block something that is falling, something light. Of course, it is tempting to point to the window because of what's going on outside, but that would be cheating. I present the invisible object again, firmly held in my right hand. Then, I bring my left hand close to the right one and raise my left hand as my right-hand tilts up.

I crawl under my invisible protection, periodically poking my head out, looking up at the sky. I even do a little dance, like I'm Charlie Chaplin, which is convenient on account of the little square of a mustache he has. I nearly go to my lips to mimic it but stop. Don't confuse things, I think. The crowd in front of me is so brilliant, so historically in tune, they don't need any extra clues. They might actually backfire, insulting them, and we can't have that on my debut night into society. There's no need to goose-step or throw my right arm up at a 45-degree angle. That'd be crass. They know what my word is and what I'm talking about.

This has been easy. After all, I could have been given the Emu War. That would have been embarrassing and tarnished my respectability. Fortunately, all I've had to do is mimic using the title of this chapter for people to get to the A-word.

"Appeasement!" they cry out in merriment. Cue applause.

But scratch that. Too easy. Let's start over, shall we?

Let's say I've been given a person as my task instead.

Two fingers go up. "Two words!" sings the crowd.

In many ways, it is the same as before. I pantomime the umbrella and poke my head out to examine the imaginary rain. I refrain from goose-stepping but add just a little extra piece: I plaster my hair down on my forehead and give myself an overbite that would impress a beaver. It only takes a minute.

"Chamberlain!" everyone shouts.

Yes! Yes! I nod. But wait, mates, we're not done. I motion with my hands. I need more. More, more! People look at one another puzzled, perhaps not knowing that the Chamberlain is a common enough name and that it just so happens that the Chamberlain we're trying to locate had multiple relatives famous enough to include in a game of charades – if you're in England, at least.

Finally, they get what I'm after.

"*Neville!*" they shout. "Neville *Chamberlain.*"

They're quite chuffed about their joint discovery.

Yes, I say, *Neville Chamberlain.* How clever of you all! Absolutely smashing! Not *Joseph* Chamberlain, his father, the great orator, and reformer who bounced around the political spectrum when he wasn't making jack manufacturing screws. Not his brother, *Austen* Chamberlain, a major statesman who won the Nobel Peace Prize for negotiating the Locarno Pact (um... that one did not age so well, truth be told). No, we're talking about Neville, whose reputation, by comparison, has been rather savagely beaten over the years. He is married to the A word – sorry, I mean – and I think we all know this: *appeasement.* And by appeasement, we mean what everyone learns in high school so that they might be able to fling it at somebody later in life. Because appeasement, in Neville's case, is his mollification of Adolf Hitler at Munich, his naïve belief that the Teutonic bully could be placated with concessions – when, in fact, they only fed his hunger till all of a sudden jackbooted Nazis were gobbling pierogies in Poland.

As I hold forth on the Chamberlain family, I cannot help but notice that the elation of the crowd has worn off a bit. They all seem to be waiting for me to stop talking. After all, this is a game of charades. At the same time, this *is* my six-million-pound townhouse, they're drinking *my* expensive sherry. And so am I. In fact, maybe it's the sherry that has loosened my tongue up because I'm into my third glass and need to talk. I don't really care much about the crowd's displeasure. (I presume the sherry is delightful; I wonder what it tastes like.)

I keep talking about Neville. I tell them that this Chamberlain has been dragged through the mud for almost a century and probably has an eternity of additional mud-dragging to look forward to. Did he commit genocide? No. Did he purge his political opponents? Again, no. Did he have a mistress, murder his wife, abscond with a bag full of quid? No, no, and no.

A monster like Lenin grimly festers under glass in Moscow as people line up to take selfies with his melting corpse. Ruthless Robespierre peeks out impishly from his terra cotta likeness in Vizille with impunity. But don't go looking for memorials of the Coroner – Neville's nickname, by the way – even before Munich, if you can believe it.

In the National Gallery, you'll find a bust of his half-brother Sir (knighted!) Austen. But there's only a medallion for Neville, probably stuck in storage and coated in dust. Visit Westminster Abbey, and you can marvel at the bust of his father, but Neville only has his name etched in a stone on the ground, something to step on. If you're determined to honor the man, as I have been, you're relegated to eBay, locating a ceramic cup of Neville's head with an umbrella as its handle. I paid 35 quid, plus shipping costs, only to be underwhelmed by its size when it arrived. Perhaps it's not a teacup at all. Perhaps it's for cream.

I walk over to a bookshelf where the Chamberlain cup sits, walk back before the crowd, and show it to them.

"You tell me. Is this for tea or cream?"

And now, I really notice it: the fashionable crowd of Londoners is quite cheesed off about my soliloquy. They won't say anything, probably because they want continued access to my eight-million-pound mansion and my expensive sherry, but it's obvious. They think my Neville speech is a load of tosh.

They sit silently before me. A few people on the carpet shift their weight uncomfortably. One person sitting on the couch seems quite cross. His name is Leo, a real hothead who flies into frequent rages. Unfortunately, he has a lot of social capital in these parts. So, when he angrily jumps up from the couch and leaves the room denouncing my bloviation, I know I'm in big trouble, my social prospects dimming before my eyes. I've spent ten million pounds on this townhouse, nearly the entirety of the advance for this book, and here I've alienated someone who can positively ruin me in this town. I need to think fast.

I find him in the vestibule as he angrily rifles through a forest of brollies sprouting from my enormously elegant umbrella stand. He won't even look at me as I attempt to apologize for monopolizing the game of charades. "It's charades!!!" He yells. "In charades, you are SILENT!!! SILENCE is what charades is about!!!"

He's really screaming now, and I'm worried what my other guests might think. I tell him he's right, of course, charades are about silence. Believe me, it won't happen again.

In fact, look, I won't even take another turn. I'll just be in the crowd, guessing as other people go. Please stay.

He says nothing, but he pauses his search for his brolly.

Look, I say, you run the night. I'll just be one of the group.

It's not good enough for him. He has demands, a whole list of them. For one, yes, he will indeed run charades from now on, thank you very much. But he also wants to decide what else happens during the night. And he might need to spread out. The living room is too small for some of his games. So, expect to relinquish control of the kitchen for sure and maybe other parts of the house. And another thing: the night ends when he says it ends. Too many of these parties are cut short. As far as Leo's concerned, it's not a party unless it's a total party.

By now, I feel like there's no alternative. In a way, he's already in charge. Why not make it official? We return to the living room, and I inform the other guests of the new order of things. They seem relieved that we have come to a peaceful solution; though, like me, they are probably apprehensive of what it all means.

From there, everything goes to hell lightning fast. Five hours later, I found myself hiding in a small bathroom on the second floor. I retreated from the first floor well before midnight, just after Leo initiated a game that demanded pitch darkness. Guests began lunging around the rooms, overturning furniture in their blindness, figurines, and pieces of China crashing down on the ground. All the while, the music has grown louder. The bass thumping is awful, and I hear muted yells from downstairs; I cannot tell if they're joyful or tragic. I'm wondering where the bobbies are. Surely, a party this out of control would alarm the neighbors, and they would call the authorities and all the chaos would stop.

People are on the second floor now. They're not making noise, just quietly running around, which makes it all the more terrifying. Maybe if I can get out of the bathroom, I can find a safe place. Perhaps on the third floor.

Yeah, it might be time to go check out the third floor.

AND SUDDENLY, we are awake. Leo and that Kensington townhouse is just a bad dream now. Thank God! We're back in a high school in America, just a normal school churning out a quality educational experience every weekday. Let's call it John F. Kennedy Memorial High, a medium-sized school with 1,200 students, linoleum halls, and fluorescent-lit classrooms. Safe and sound. We're in a 20th-century history class. It's the first class of the day, and the students are sleepy. Actually, some are not just sleepy; they're asleep, faces planted on their desks. One is beginning to leak a mucus trail. Even my eagerest beavers seem to be hibernating.

"Hitler," I declare, knowing this is a name that usually wakes them up. I explain how there was this fella Neville Chamberlain who was the Prime Minister of the United Kingdom, and in 1938, in Munich, he quite foolishly attempted to negotiate with Hitler. That's right, *Hitler*. *Adolf* Hitler. The *Nazi*.

Everyone knows you can't trust *Hitler*, right?

My students slowly awaken, nodding sagely. Of course not.

I tell them that Adolf makes all these demands and promises to this guy Chamberlain, and that for some reason, Neville believes him. But of course, Hitler breaks all his promises and invades a bunch of countries in the process. If only this guy Neville had stood up to him and said, "No way, Dolfie," we wouldn't even have had a World War 2. It would have just been World War 1 with no sequel. Sequels may be fun to watch, but 75 million dead people is a drag.

So obviously, Hitler makes this guy Neville look like a world-class idiot. He could have stopped Hitler in Munich just by saying no, and instead, he caved. In fact, I tell my students that Chamberlain might be the biggest idiot of the 20th century. His name is now synonymous with weakness, giving in, and appeasing Hitler. Such a wimp.

A special kind of contempt is reserved for this kind of equivocator, probably because his example is so useful for us. If we ever get mad at someone for not being aggressive, we can just say they're like Chamberlain. You can see how super useful this is. It turns what might be an overly aggressive piece of warmongering into a highly principled, world-saving stance. Pretty neat.

"That's what Neville said to Hitler," we might say scornfully when critiquing someone's weak negotiating style. Or "Sounds like you'd be comfortable making deals in Munich," to those unable to set boundaries. If we're really being annoying, we might pantomime the opening of an umbrella and dance around like Charlie Chaplin, alternatively goose-stepping and throwing up Nazi salutes. Because we're not in stuffy Kensington now. We can be our annoying selves.

Speaking of which, I notice my students' attention is flagging again. Perhaps I haven't dropped Hitler's name enough to keep them awake. But I have an idea. I walk over to the closet, poke my head in, and come out with an umbrella.

"What's this?" I ask, holding it up for them.

They're not in the mood. They stare sullenly.

"Seriously, what's this?" I insist.

"An umbrella," says Marco grudgingly.

"Yeah," I say, "or what the British call a brolly."

I hold it in my right hand and wield it like a sword, swooshing it through the air and almost knocking Marie's backpack off her desk. This gets their attention. Then, I do something way more radical, bringing my left hand down to the step and unsnapping the retaining strap. The umbrella flutters a bit, now unrestricted. They are suddenly awake to the threat I present to them, and it makes me smile – a big, crazy smile. Now they're awake. They know I can't be trusted at times like these. I'm the kind of teacher who does dumb things like double-stepping on a student's foot. They don't want any part of what comes next. Besides, they're a superstitious bunch. Everyone knows it's bad luck to open an umbrella inside.

"Hold on," protests Marie in the front row.

Evan, in the back row, stands up, hands outstretched. "Coady, don't."

Making teenagers suffer is a sideline of mine. It makes up for the low wages and mind-numbing curriculum meetings. So, yes, I'm loving this, every second of it. With my left hand, I begin to ever so gently pull back and forth on the umbrella stem, just an inch up, then an inch back, so the black umbrella flaps like a giant bat. Now, I have their full attention. A few of them are up out of their seats.

That's bad luck, Coady. We don't need bad luck, thank you very much. We don't mess with this kind of thing, Coady, we don't tempt fate.

But they know I do. All the time.

"Do you dare me?" I say, flapping the umbrella. "Do you dare me?"

They're all awake now.

I RAN the umbrella around the room gleefully, gently flapping its wings but not fully opening it while my students got caught up in the frenzy. What might have, at first, been merely a faint protest to the supposed bad luck of an umbrella being opened inside quickly reached a fever pitch. It was quite hysterical – for them, emotionally – for me, humorously. But they're ready to work now.

They've agreed to my terms, which is that we have 45 minutes left in class, and we're going to spend it awake and working. We have three political cartoons of Neville Chamberlain that feature his umbrella, and we need to do a full workup. I point out that they have just appeased me, and they tell me they're not in the mood. Coady, don't push your luck. They're all pale and clammy and just want to get out of the class with their fortunes intact.

They have the cartoons laid out before them on a sheet of paper.

"What's with all the umbrellas?" Kai wants to know.

"Chamberlain always carried one. It was his signature style."

"You mean, like, his brand?" they say.

"Sure, his brand. So, what's the brand?"

"Well," they tell me, "It's very British, right? It can be a cane when it's not raining. It is also like a sword; you could use it as a weapon in a pinch."

"Yes," I say, "but what does it do?"

Duh, Coady, it blocks rain. Right, I say. So, it keeps you protected. And if you carry it all the time it means you're always ready for the unexpected. They decide they like the brand. It seems cool for a leader, particularly a British one.

"Fair enough," I say, picking back up the umbrella, which is now strapped tight again. I cut the air with it. "But it may be a double-edged sword."

I project the first of three political cartoons on the front board.

Chamberlain is on a fraying tightrope, his umbrella open, probably to give him balance, but he doesn't look very balanced. One foot is up, and he doesn't want to put it down because if he does, he'll step on the most frayed part of the rope. So, he's suspended in suspense and looks very unsure of himself and worried, especially as beneath him there are rows of bayonets alongside the Italian and Nazi flag. On one side of this chasm is a stake with a tag reading, "appeasement;" on the other side, there is a Japanese soldier grinning wickedly. The soldier has a knife in his hand, and the implication is clear: it would take very little to break this frayed rope, which is helpfully marked "British Prestige." And if that happens, Chamberlain, and probably England, will be finished.

The class likes the action in this one. It's clear that Chamberlain's policy of appeasement has put England in a tenuous position. Because of appeasement, their prestige is thinning to the point of breaking. All it would take is something with Japan to make that happen. As for the umbrella, they're not sure. They see it as useful for Neville to keep his balance, but they figure there's more to it. Sarah says he wouldn't need to balance if it weren't for the tightrope, and the tightrope is attached to appeasement. So, the umbrella shouldn't be necessary, but here it is, and it also makes Chamberlain look stupid like a clown.

They think the second cartoon makes Chamberlain look like a clown, too. In this one, he has an umbrella open, but there's no rain; it's horizontal, tucked under his arm. Neville looks a bit messy – a little bit like a tramp. Or a clown. In his back pocket, he has a rolled-up document that reads, "My guarantee of the Czech frontier," and beyond that, there is a tiny Hitler holding a piece of the Earth marked "CZECH." He's lopping off pieces with a long knife. At the top, there's a sentence: "What a handy article an umbrella is."

The students don't love this one. A bit obvious, they sniff. They also don't think it's clear why Chamberlain has an umbrella or why it's supposed to be handy. They look a little closer and see that Chamberlain is looking up at the sky, supposedly to see if it's raining. So, he's distracted. Hitler is in the background going to stabbytown on Czechoslovakia while Chamberlain, with an open umbrella, seems more concerned about rain that isn't even there. So, that makes sense. They like it a little more now, but it's not their favorite. That's the next one.

It's titled "Lost Face," and sure enough, the main figure, clearly Chamberlain striding forward, has no face. It is not even drawn in. But the faces of Hitler and a Japanese soldier, maybe Hirohito, look on gleefully, pointing at Chamberlain mockingly. Chamberlain's umbrella is being used like a cane and is tied together with a tag reading "BRITISH DIPLOMACY." Meanwhile, Chamberlain is pulling a snarling lion who is reluctant to move forward.

The students like this one a lot. For one, it's well-drawn. But they also think it's the most cutting of the three. After all, what's worse than not even having a face? It's the worst kind of thing you could say about someone.

"Yeah," says Evan, "I'd rather be hated than invisible."

It's tempting to point out that we all know this about him.

Marie wants to know if it means anything that the

umbrella is closed in this cartoon. In the others, the umbrella is opened.

"I don't know," says Kai. "Is it saying that British diplomacy is preventing it from being opened? As Coady said, an umbrella is protection."

I shrug. They may be taking the symbolism a bit too far.

"Whatever it is," says Kai, "this guy Chamberlain has got no face."

True, I tell them and then explain to them that losing face is an old-fashioned term for losing respectability. Annoyed, they informed me that they already knew that. In any case, they begin to see now just how reviled Neville became. Initially, they liked the umbrella as part of Chamberlain's brand. Now, they think it's a mistake. They can see why some politicians try so hard to be bland. I tell them that, in fact, Eisenhower and Nixon – two bland but effective presidents – made sure never to be photographed under an umbrella.

"So, this guy Chamberlain," says Sarah. "What happened to him?"

"Died in November of 1940."

Karim, who's the real history buff in the room, groans. He knows the implication of the date: Chamberlain died at one of the bleakest moments of the war, after the evacuation at Dunkirk and just one month into the Nazi bombing of England, the Blitz. He may well have passed away listening to distant explosions of his own making. He died not knowing whether the Nazis would be ultimately stopped, and England would rise from the ashes.

The class takes a silent moment to take in his sad passing.

"Wow," says Kai. "Talk about poetic justice."

"Yeah, he's a real goat," I say.

They're confused. How is he the goat, Coady? That's a good thing like Tom Brady or Michael Jordan. I say no, a goat is a bad thing, someone blamed for losing the game. They take pity on me, explaining that today goat means Greatest of All Time. Jay comes up and writes it on the board: G.O.A.T.

Yeah, well, I tell them, when I was growing up it meant someone you blamed for losing, like a scapegoat. Neville is definitely that kind of goat.

"But, like, in the biggest way," says Sarah.

"So, maybe he's the G.O.A.T at being the goat," suggests Marie.

I turn to the board: Neville = G.O.A.T. of goats.

But guess what, I tell the class. There's someone who disgraced himself even more than Neville in this whole affair. Hard to believe, I know. And this might surprise you more: he was an American. And guess what! You know his last name. Because you see this name every day at least 20 times; though, you may not recognize his first name. He's quite a character.

He actually makes poor disgraced Neville look good.

Joseph P. Kennedy. You might know him better as Jack's dad. Or Bobby's dad. Or, if you're really into history and have seen the movie where the car runs off the little bridge in Martha's

Vineyard and the Kennedy in question runs from it while a woman drowns, Teddy's dad. Joe is the patriarch of the family, the driving force who makes a fortune through stock speculation, Hollywood studios, and supposedly but not probably conspiring with the mob to control the liquor rackets during Prohibition. He's a remarkably dynamic character. On balance, he's a dedicated father – though a terrible philanderer – and has bootstrapped himself from humble East Boston to become a national figure with political aspirations. He's an American success story.

He's also a terrific pain in the ass.

He supports Franklin Roosevelt for president, and in return, he is appointed first as the Chairman of the Security and Exchange Commission, then later as Chairman of the U.S. Maritime Commission. He proves effective in these roles, and his political aspirations grow, not-so-quietly hoping Roosevelt won't run for a third term in 1940. This is perhaps why Roosevelt, definitely running for a third term in 1940, selects Joe to be the American Ambassador to the Court of St. James (that is, to England).

It's an improbable choice. Kennedy lacks experience and is undiplomatic by nature. He's also Boston Irish, which will not please the Protestant blue bloods of London (a tough crowd – trust me, I know). But for Roosevelt, it has the benefit of keeping this terrific pain in the ass on the other side of the Atlantic and away from the press.

Unfortunately for Franklin, Joe manages to be such a terrific pain in the ass that he attracts the press from all the way across the Atlantic. In London, Kennedy pushes to get a meeting with Hitler, apparently in an attempt to mollify the dictator. In the process, he spouts off some anti-Semitic rhetoric, perhaps intended to prove his credentials to the German Ambassador. These leak to the press and cause problems for the Roosevelt administration.

Kennedy, at heart, does not want a war. Perhaps this is because his sons are of an age where they would serve; perhaps it is because war would mess with his business interests. Whatever the case, he falls in with Chamberlain's crowd, a group that Roosevelt, back in Washington, does not want to be associated with. But Joe doesn't care what Roosevelt wants and imagines that the ambassadorship gives him carte blanche to pursue policies he thinks are best for America.

He goes all in on appeasement, believing Germany's moves are really about opening up new markets as opposed to creating a master race that will enslave humanity. He is not much of a reader or an ideologue. He is an opportunist, a man of action, and above all, a businessman – and not the kind of business set up to profit off war. Even his anti-Semitism is mostly tribal; generally speaking, he is an equal-opportunity bigot, and for all his world travels, he remains a kid from East Boston, trying to get bigger and bigger by putting everybody else down.

Only, from here on out, he will get smaller and smaller. Because, as we know, Hitler breaks his promises to Chamberlain, consuming Czechoslovakia in the process. Even old Neville the Coroner is sobered, renouncing his policies, and meekly handing power to Churchill. Appeasement is dead and buried.

But not for Joe. He digs it back up, suggesting Germany be paid not to invade Poland. Ludicrous. When the Luftwaffe bombs London in the Blitz, Joe leaves the city to avoid the explosions and earns the nickname "Jittery Joe" in the press. Even then, however, Joe sticks to his (metaphorical) guns. He claims Hitler was lured into the war having been denied his proper market share. He makes inflammatory remarks about democracy being toast in England and suggests America cook up some fascism of their own if they have any hope of surviving what comes next.

So, now he is no longer just a terrific pain in the ass; he is a full-on car crash. Roosevelt holds him in England mainly to keep his big mouth out of the papers. When Joe does return, Roosevelt invites him to dinner. There are no records of what they talk about at that dinner, but some claim Roosevelt gives his wayward ex-ambassador an ultimatum: *Get yourself out of politics, Joe, or your kids won't have a future in the Democratic Party. They won't even get elected dog catchers. Got it?*

After that, Joe goes quiet. He makes more money, but his political aspirations are now just dust in the winds of war. He places all his hopes in his eldest son, Joe Jr., who soon goes down in flames in a plane over Europe. Now his next eldest will need to fulfill all his hopes and dreams.

It's John's turn.

. . .

JOHN GETS RIGHT TO WORK. Returning from working at the embassy in London, John – what the heck, let's call him Jack – throws himself into his senior thesis at Harvard. It's about – *you guessed it* – appeasement. Apparently, this senior thesis of Jack's is noteworthy enough to find its way out of the Ivy League and into a major publishing house. Or perhaps, it's just that his father is powerful enough and happens to be close friends with publishing magnate Henry Luce, but Jack's work finds a favorable landing. Jack's thesis is also greatly burnished by Arthur Krock, Pulitzer Prize-winning journalist and New York Times bureau chief in Washington. It is renamed from *Appeasement in Munich* to *Why England Slept*. A snappy cover is plastered on the book and guess what? It becomes an instant bestseller. How annoying is that?

It's the beginning of a long run of mythmaking around JFK that persists to this day. The cornerstones of Camelot are laid as proud Joe works his connections and cronies to transform a thin thesis into a well-reviewed tome that boosts his son's national profile. What the book posits is also convenient for Joe: Jack asserts that Chamberlain's appeasement of Hitler was a foregone conclusion. In reality, Neville was in charge of an England that was neither militarily nor psychologically prepared for the cost of war. And so, while Jack's book does not endorse appeasement, it slyly deflates it, relegating it to a lesser transgression, looking instead at structural elements laid well in advance.

Now, all of this could be cynically seen as a shallow canard, but here's the thing: his thesis is sound. There were in fact structural issues holding Chamberlain in place. He was a democratically elected politician, not a dictator who could drop on the ground and chew the carpet. He lived in the shadow of the Great Depression and the Great War. He served a public that was largely desperate for just the kind of agreement he brought home. Appeasement bought England time, just as the Nazi-Soviet alliance bought time for Stalin (though he squandered it). If anyone had the right to be miffed, it was France, but they were a mess leading up to the war and largely responsible for the rise of Hitler in the first place, so don't waste too much sympathy there.

And so, here we have a growing vision of Chamberlain as a perpetual victim of history. His flight to Munich and his appeasement of Hitler are the actions of a man whose choices have been eliminated before he can speak. Negligent politicians whose names we do not even remember have delivered disaster to his doorstep. He can do little but appease. And then, moving forward, he becomes the face of a weakness that was, by and large, not his own. How terrifically wicked of history.

Jack may be the first to come to Chamberlain's historical defense, attempting to free Neville from the wreckage of his scorned legacy. Who knows, perhaps Chamberlain got a chance to read it as it was published a few months before his death. If he did, he could not possibly know that these would be the words of a future president who would also be trapped under the wreckage of history.

Krock and others may have helped with the manuscript,

but Jack did manage a lot of the heavy lifting required by the book. While he profited from unfettered access to research through his connections to the American Embassy in London, he also produced a decent piece of revisionist history in almost real-time. And that's the thing about JFK: for all the mythmaking, there is something real and admirable at his core. He is a genuine sophisticate, a gentle person, and an actual thinker. He is not the volcanic success and disaster that is his father. He is a young man of frail health who tries every which way to join the war effort despite a ruined back. Myths will be spun from his service, but those too are based in reality. He behaved heroically and altruistically in the Pacific.

And when his book about appeasement becomes a bestseller, he does the right thing. Profits from the British sales are donated to the city of Plymouth, recently hit hard by the Luftwaffe. (Profits from the American publication are another matter, however. With that money, he buys a Buick.)

It's a convertible. The umbrella of automobiles.

PRESIDENT JOHN FITZGERALD KENNEDY is in a convertible. Not a Buick this time, a Lincoln. He is seated in the back next to his wife, Jacqueline, who is wearing pink. In front of him is Governor John Connally and his wife, Nellie. As a northern liberal member of the Democratic party, he can't expect too warm of a reception here deep in the heart of Texas. Just a month earlier, Adlai Stevenson had been spat on, and in 1960, even Texan Vice President Lyndon Johnson and his wife, Ladybird, had been attacked by an angry mob in Dallas when entering their hotel. So, this is hostile territory. Indeed, Kennedy is mostly here to smooth over bad blood within the state's Democratic party. This is a mission of mercy and unity.

The motorcade route is designed for maximum exposure. Every additional mile means tens of thousands of happy customers, and it is those happy customers that will keep the party together and Texas firmly in the Democratic Party's grasp. And so, the convertible top is down. Years before, a young Jack might have been tooling around in Cambridge with his Buick, top-down, cruising for pretty girls. Now, he has a beautiful and beloved wife, and he is living the dream of his father, who is back in Hyannis, incoherent after a massive stroke.

Later, some people – and by some people, I mean conspiracists – will wonder why in the world they had the top down in a hostile city like Dallas, but the entire point of the tour was to be seen by as many people as possible. You must give the people what they want if you want what they have. In this case, votes.

This is not the same kind of morning that Caesar experienced on the Ides of March. Jackie did not wake up inconsolable after having a dream of holding a dead husband in her arms. Jack did not dream of rising above the clouds and shaking the hand of Jupiter, though there is a morbid anti-Kennedy ad in the morning paper. No jackass like Spurinna lurks in the shadows making spooky noises. Hardened skeptics might draw a comparison between Lyndon Johnson and Decimus, believing that Kennedy's trip to Texas was a lure to get him shot – threshing the birds out of the bush so to speak – but if it was, Governor John Connally, in the front seat, who will also be shot, was not in on it.

Et tu, Lyndon?

Et tu? What in the goddamn hell is "et tu"? That ballet or something?

As they move from Love Field through the suburbs of Dallas, they are met with relatively thin crowds. But the cheers grow louder and build into a fever pitch as they enter the city center. Kennedy may have been concerned about his standing in Dallas before, but he is not now. In fact, a little bit later, just as they turn into Dealey Plaza, Nellie Connally will turn back to Jack and say, "Mr. President, they can't make you believe now that there are not some in Dallas who love and appreciate you, can they?" It is a mangled question, filled with negatives that mean positives, and it is hard to answer. It is the kind of question that could only spring from Texas, a place whose elaborate courtesy masks the violence beneath. Kennedy, quick on his feet, follows her well enough, saying, "No, they can't."

They'll be the last words he ever speaks.

But hold on: we're not there yet. Kennedy is still in downtown Dallas, enjoying the crowd, maybe thinking about how badly he is going to thump Goldwater in next year's election. Maybe thinking about his dad up in Hyannis Port who has been immobilized by a stroke, or who knows? Perhaps ruminating on his older brother Joe Jr. whose plane broke up in the skies over Europe. Joe Jr. was supposed to be president. But then Hitler invaded Czechoslovakia then Poland, and before you knew it, there was a war. It's funny how things work out.

Around this time, Louie Steven Witt gets up from his desk at the Rio Grande Insurance Company on the corner of Elm and Field Street. He goes to the coat rack and picks up his umbrella. He has a plan and goes down to the street. He walks south on Field Street over to Main Street, seeing a crowd forming in anticipation of Kennedy's motorcade. He heads west on Main. There are fewer people in this direction, so he heads there.

To do what he needs to do, he doesn't want a crowd. He takes a left down Houston Street then goes north on Elm Street, back toward the direction where he started. So, he's kind of walking in a circle, a bit directionless. He's probably nervous. Is he holding his umbrella horizontally by his waist, or is he using it like a cane? We don't know. But walking down Elm Street he comes into Dealey Plaza, and he makes his way down where there are very few people.

There's a grassy incline in this part and a wall behind that. Behind that wall, there are train tracks. We don't know if Witt ever felt strange in this space. Did he know history was about to change?

Finally, he comes to a stop. He can hear the cheering

coming from a few blocks away and must know Kennedy is closing in on where he has set up. He has his plan and knows what he has to do. It makes him uncomfortable, and it is out of character, but now, he is ready and in position. He waits.

Kennedy's Lincoln is on Houston Street, taking a left on Elm.

We're back in my classroom on the first floor of John F. Kennedy Memorial High. It's a month after the lesson with the umbrella. They remember Chamberlain and appeasement but not much about Joe Kennedy and his son Jack's senior thesis. This is despite the fact that Kennedy's profile is on the stationary, and JFK is plastered across their sports uniforms, hoodies, and social media accounts.

They'll graduate soon enough and tell each other "JFK for life!" and move into their futures remembering these days fondly. Maybe they'll recall the time Coady threatened them with an umbrella, and altogether forget that for most of their years here in these hallowed halls, they claimed J.F.K. stood for Jail For Kids. Without what is about to go down in Dealey Plaza, none of this branding would be in place. History would have been altogether different. Who knows what this place would be called without this sacrifice in Dallas?

But it is called JFK, and consequently, the students feel a sense of ownership and pride – and protectiveness – for Kennedy. And now I am painting them a picture of November 22, 1963, and they know something bad is about to happen to our namesake. There's also this guy Louie Steven Witt that Coady is talking about. Witt seems to be walking in circles with an umbrella, and they can't figure him out. As Kennedy weaves through Dallas at 20 miles per hour, and Witt strolls down the sidewalk to find a thin crowd along the route, they are on the edge of their seats. They know what is next, but they can't look away. Just like you.

I have my umbrella in my hands again. It's firmly strapped tight, and I've been walking back and forth in front of them, pretending to be Witt. They are a bit mesmerized, particularly by the umbrella; although, I can't help but notice Karim has his laptop open. This is pretty common, and he's often scouring the Internet for info on what I'm talking about in real time.

I call him the Googleman, a knowledgeable boogeyman who haunts their history teacher. It's a bit of a horse race between the two of us, and I can only win by dodging, misdirecting, and bringing topics to a full stop. Googleman sometimes catches up and bites me in the ass, and the only way to get him off it is to admit I don't know, or better still, that I'm not sure. Yes, Coady, tell them that you're not sure. If you're really worried about what they think, tell them it is impossible to know for sure. No one can. At the same time, the Googleman might bail me out. It's happened before. I can just look at Karim during a lecture and have him say, "Yeah, it says here..." Already, today, Karim has added a few interesting facts to our conversation, including the detail that it was raining the morning of the assassination. I let the Googleman be.

I walk them through the final minutes, bringing Kennedy and Witt closer.

Kennedy is rounding Dealey Plaza, folks. The bulk of the goodwill is behind him now. But Nellie Connally turns back to him and asks him her tortured question: "Mr. President, they can't make you believe now that there are not some in Dallas who love and appreciate you, can they?" And it is at this moment that Louie Witt steps forward toward the motorcade.

In class, I step forward with the umbrella. They grow wary.

And Kennedy approaches in the Lincoln convertible.

I unsnap the umbrella strap. They look apprehensive.

And Witt brings his right hand down to the umbrella.

I bring my right hand down to the umbrella stem.

And Kennedy is now just feet away from Witt.

I take a firm hold of the metal ring inside the sheath of the umbrella.

And then...

I take a sharp breath and get ready.

And then...

I look at them. They're all eyes.

And then...

In one violent motion, I open the umbrella while swinging it over my head. It sends just the slightest breeze through the room, but that breeze feels like a shockwave. The kids are stunned. Their eyes are wide, and they're confused.

And here I am with an open umbrella in the classroom, again.

I motion up with my eyes at the umbrella, questioningly.

But they say nothing.

"Aren't you guys mad?" I ask.

"What?" they wonder.

"The umbrella," I say, "I opened it in class. Aren't you guys mad I opened it in class?" I gently bounce the umbrella up and down over my head.

They are both confused and contemptuous.

"What are you talking about?" says Kai, clearly upset.

"What?" I say, confused and a bit alarmed. I realize that they're angry at me all of a sudden. Sure, teenagers are fickle, just ask anyone. But these teens have never been like this. They're a strange stew of feelings, and I can't quite figure out all the flavors.

"Whoa," says Evan in the back, "Whoa. What just happened?"

If my taste buds are right, they're pissed off at me but not about opening the umbrella. It's almost like they're annoyed that I'm even suggesting they would be mad about that. Here we are, our beloved JFK is about to be shot, you got this guy over here opening an umbrella for God knows what reasons – and you're asking us what? Whether we're mad because you opened an umbrella in class?

"What happened?" says Marie, almost despondent.

I shrug. "What do you mean? Kennedy got shot."

"At that very moment?"

"Yeah, at that moment."

"When this guy opens the umbrella?" she asks, perplexed.

Uh-huh, yes. He got shot when Witt opened the umbrella.

"Coady," says Evan, taking a deep breath, clearly trying to contain a volcanic level of annoyance beneath. "You're a good guy, and I don't want this to sound disrespectful, but what the hell are you talking about?"

Kai agrees. "What does it all mean?"

Holy shit! What does it all mean? They're asking me what it all means. Oh boy, this is bad. I'm in front of a class with an open umbrella, a middle-aged, middle-class, loving but sometimes wayward history teacher, and they want to know what it all means. They feel screwed. They want answers.

I look around the room, and they all look like they've seen a ghost. Except for the Googleman. Karim is smiling; the deathly blue and white glow of his laptop on his face gives him a ghoulish look. He knows. He's been furiously clacking away on the keyboard during my display, and he knows. Usually, I'm worried about him biting my ass, but now, he's going to save it. Looking to get out of the line of fire, I point to the Googleman: "Ask Karim," I say. "Karim knows."

He'll tell you.

KARIM EXPLAINS that Witt's umbrella was a protest, a reference to appeasement. Because, as we know, an umbrella can represent appeasement. We also know that Joe Kennedy was the worst appeaser of them all and that he made Chamberlain look reasonable by comparison. Remember how he wanted to pay Germany not to invade Poland? Totally nuts.

And what you may or may not know, but the Googleman knows by swimming in the slipstream of the Internet, is that plenty of people at the time thought Jack was soft on communism, that he was a new kind of appeaser himself, that he should have invaded Cuba when he had the chance during the Bay of Pigs invasion. So, opening up an umbrella like this along the parade route is a silent protest against the Kennedys.

But you'd have to know your history to reach this conclusion. Otherwise, you might become convinced that the umbrella is a signal to assassinate Kennedy or even that there's a gun in there or some kind of poison dart. Years of your life could be flushed down the toilet trying to find the identity of the "Umbrella Man." The Umbrella Man would haunt your dreams then your waking hours. You would slowly drift into the realm of the unwell. Friends and neighbors would give you a wide berth until your spouse, too, leaves you, and your kids know you only as Dad the Fanatic. Your life is ruined because you were trying to be so very clever – but you weren't clever enough to look at the history of the moment and find out that umbrellas had been used before during Kennedy's appearances to try to shame him for his family's appeasement tendencies. But the Googleman knows.

I add a few pieces. Louie Steven Witt was not a very political man, but he considered himself a "conservative type fellow." He was not a "joiner" and didn't like to stand out. But in Arizona, a protestor had opened an umbrella to protest the President, and apparently, this gesture annoyed Kennedy. Witt heard about this during a coffee break and "never thinking too much of liberal politics" decided to do something out of character. He grabbed his umbrella and made for the parade route, looking for a place without many people, mostly because he was not the kind of person to cause a scene.

Then, he opened up his umbrella as Kennedy passed. That was it. Witt didn't even see Kennedy getting shot. Why? Because he was opening his damn umbrella. We know this because 15 years later, after voluminous speculation on the Umbrella Man that Witt was oblivious to, Congress finally found and subpoenaed him. In 1978, before the United States House Select Committee on Assassinations, he self-effacingly explained his movements on the day in question, November 22, 1963.

So, the umbrella meant nothing, at least in terms of Kennedy's death. It's only proof that, if you look at any event closely, you'll see all kinds of weird things. Those weird things can form a constellation from which you can build meaning, but most of it is meaningless. And that is too bad. Because, though I won't tell the students this, I'm personally inclined to believe Kennedy was killed by a cabal with ties in the government and organized crime. But things like the umbrella just happen to obscure that.

In fact, there's some evidence that the conspiracy against

Kennedy, if it existed, thrived not on containing the truth but on unleashing multiple truths. Randomness. Because when you're chasing false leads, you often find yourself stuck in dead ends. If the conspirators did, in fact, exist, they sure must have loved the unexpected arrival of Umbrella Man, a tasty freebie on their journey of removing their enemy from the face of the Earth. Conspiracies love crackpots.

Now, there are 15 minutes left in class, and I tell them to get their computers out and open YouTube. Excited, they pop the lids of their laptops, and over the din, I instruct them to find examples of umbrellas in crowds where there's a president. Two points extra credit to whoever finds the best example.

Karim finds a good clip in under a minute. It is from the morning of the assassination at the airport in Fort Worth. Kennedy is about to take a 15-minute flight to Dallas instead of taking a 30-minute drive. Because remember, the whole trip to Texas is a big show, an attempt to bring unity to the Texas Democratic Party. Kennedy is not going to deprive Dallas of a proper Air Force One landing. Were he to do so, Dallas might get mad at Fort Worth, and certain news anchors of certain news stations would certainly be unhappy.

Umbrellas are everywhere. Dozens of opened umbrellas. But while some conspiracy theorists might fall down a rabbit hole of speculation, attempting to identify a host of umbrella-wielding grandmothers, the explanation is a lot simpler: it's raining. There's nothing suspicious about an umbrella in the rain. It's only the umbrella at rest or the umbrella in the sun –

the dreaded parasol – that piques our interest. But Karim thinks it's interesting that it was raining the morning of Kennedy's assassination, and he found out the Secret Service had prepared the bubble to be put atop the Lincoln convertible. Alas, it stopped raining by mid-morning. The bubble was left off, and history was never the same.

Evan finds a clip from September 5, 1968. It's a Nixon campaign stop in Chicago. Along the route, up against the barricade, a young blond woman holds an open umbrella. There's no rain, and it's not sunny, so there's no reason to have it open. It's blocking the view of people behind her, but either they are, as Midwesterners, too polite to complain, or this woman is too deaf to hear them. Evan thinks it's special because it's a red umbrella. He wonders, in a very Evan type of way, who in the hell would buy a red umbrella in the first place, but the rest of us are not moved by this searing insight. In any case, it is not a signal for Nixon's assassination, red or not. They'll get Nixon by other means.

But Marie finds the best one: September 12, 1962, when Kennedy is in Texas to visit Rice University and gives his "We choose to go to the moon" speech. It's a year before his assassination but very much the same scene and very much in Texas. During this motorcade, Kennedy stands in the back seat of the Lincoln, presenting himself as an easy target to the long rows of tall buildings on either side. It's a beautiful, sunny day with puffy white clouds, not a raindrop in sight. But along the route, unmistakably, someone has a big black umbrella open. They're blocking people's view of the President, but they are not, as far as we know, signaling an assassination. Bad manners but not homicidal.

"Close your computers," I say. We just have a few minutes left.

"So, what do we think?"

"So, are you saying people spent years thinking this guy was part of the assassination?" says Kai.

"Yup, that's what I'm saying."

"Because he opened an umbrella?"

"That's right. At the moment of the assassination."

"Well," says Marie, "it's all so random."

"You say that like it's a bad thing."

"It *is*. It is a bad thing. Life shouldn't be that random."

"How about death?"

They give me a look: *Don't, Coady.*

Then, there is a stretch of silence, which is eventually broken by Evan in the back.

"You want to know what I think?" he says. He actually waits until I say, "Yes, Evan, we all very much want to know what you think," at which point he offers, "I think this guy Witt must have shit his pants."

Swearing is not generally allowed, but I give it a pass. It's something I've thought a dozen times myself: Witt must indeed have shit his pants. In fact, Witt told Congress, "I think if The Guinness Book of World Records had a category for people who were at the wrong place at the wrong time, doing the wrong thing, I would be No. 1 in that position without even a close runner-up."

Kai says, "So, he's kind of like the G.O.A.T. of randos."

"What's a rando?" I ask.

"Like a random person but a shady one."

"And goat means *greatest of all time*, Coady," says Evan snarkily.

As with the s-word, I let this minor infraction pass. After opening the umbrella in class, I owe them a few open shots. Some of them are wondering if this class period is going to jinx them. "All this talk of death and randomness and umbrellas. We have SATs this weekend, and if we do bad, it's your fault, Coady."

"Yes," I say, "It'll be my fault. Tell your parents it's my fault."

We still have five minutes left, enough time for an exit reflection. I tell them to open their notebooks, and they throw me a communal groan while I write the question on the board: *How did the symbolism of an umbrella change between Chamberlain's trip to Munich and Witt's testimony to Congress?* Despite the groans, I get some nice little pieces to read later on.

Karim plies me with a bunch of interesting facts; though, he misses the point. Evan takes a few more shots at me, pointing out that these disparate events are nowhere connected directly in the curriculum, but due to his forgiving nature, he will not mention this issue in class. But Marie really nails it, writing that the umbrella was put on a real journey, beginning as a prop of dependability and readiness then being reduced to something flimsy and cowardly, transforming it into a symbol of protest, which was then inadvertently seen as an instrument of improbable killing for 15 years, all because this guy Witt took a walk at lunch and got cute with a motorcade. Marie goes on to say that, while she doesn't like to see history as being this random, she accepts that it can be, and maybe I can go back and give them some more concrete stuff to learn in the next few weeks. Sure, Marie.

The bell rings and things still feel a bit unsteady, a little queasy, as my students file out of the classroom, wearily placing their notebooks on my desk in the front. Some of them shoot me a look like I'm some kind of sus rando. They'll probably never fully trust me again. But that's okay. You should, in fact, never trust your history teacher. Christ, I've told them that dozens of times.

They're gone, and I have a free block next, so I go for the tea kettle in the back. No more coffee for Coady. I'm allergic to the stuff. I brew the water and grab my big ceramic hug, which reads, "I LOVE MY HUSBAND." My wife got it for me in a dyslexic purchase – because it looks like I'm the one with a husband I love. In turn, I buy her a mug that reads, "I LOVE MY WIFE." We're still married.

And then, with my uncool and incorrect ceramic mug filled with uncool tea, I move out into the linoleum hall. It is transition time and dozens of students pass by me in a stream, a few periodically breaking off to ask questions.

"Can I hand in the homework late?"

"Yes, you can."

"Will I get points off?"

"Yes, you will."

Another one stops, "When can I take the quiz?"

When do you want to take the quiz?

"Friday. No, Monday. I have SATs on Saturday."

"Okay, Monday. Good luck."

"Actually, maybe Tuesday. I'll be recovering from the SATs on Monday."

"Okay, Tuesday it is."

A 9th grader heads down the hall toward me. Not a great student but a great kid. He's eyeing me mischievously, clearly wanting to connect. He holds his hand up to high-five as he passes. I'm suspicious but pretend to play along. He gets close, removes his hand, drops down, and throws a pulled punch into my gut. I figured he'd do something like that, so I smile and send my own pulled punch at his chin. He reels back, taking the imaginary blow, and is gone.

I am careful not to step on his shoes.

Chamberlain's wife drops her umbrella. Apparently, it's bad etiquette to pick up your own dropped umbrella – but not as bad etiquette as signing an agreement with Hitler.

Looks kind of sunny to be toting around a brolly while surrounded by dodgy Nazis. But Neville looks chuffed to bits to return to England and let everyone know the good news: he has signed a peace treaty that will lead to millions of deaths and destroy his own reputation forever.

Kennedy in a convertible, the umbrella of cars. The Presidency got him the Lincoln, but he bought his first convertible, a Buick, with profits from his book defending Neville Chamberlain – *Why England Slept*.

Louie Steven Witt seated on the far right of the photo, umbrella at his feet. One of the closest people to Kennedy during the assassination, he did not actually see it. Why? Because he was opening his damn umbrella. Why?
Ugh, don't ask.

9

PAPER CUP, PART 3
AUGUST 9, 2023

I'M in a white Toyota Tacoma with Florida plates on Jenness Street in a far corner of Springfield, Massachusetts. It's the end of summer, and I've driven three hours from Rhode Island and will have to drive another three back tonight unless I get run over crossing the street or shot for trespassing before then. This truck is a rental, and in a few days, I'll be flying back to Marrakech, Morocco, where I teach history at an American school. I'm up here trying to find Andre; if this trip doesn't pan out, I won't get another shot at it for a while.

My buddy, Whalen, is with me. He's also a teacher. We worked together at a different school – one where coffee cups didn't get smacked out of hands. He's my wingman. I explain what we're doing here, telling him about the coffee cup, the hallway in the morning, the play boxing, and Andre's boots.

"Wait," he says. "You hit his foot *twice*?"

"First time by accident," I say.

"You're saying the second time you did it on *purpose*?"

"I was just playing, seeing where it was going."

"What the hell were you thinking?" asks Whalen.

"You sound like my wife," I tell him crossly. I don't need to be reminded that it was idiotic. Of course, it was idiotic. If it weren't idiotic I wouldn't be sitting here ten years later in a rented Tacoma telling you this story in front of Andre's last known address. Quite frankly, Whalen, I'm keyed up.

Whalen nods and lets it drop. For the time being, at least.

I've actually been trying to connect with Andre for months. Everyone says these young kids are all over social media, but he's almost non-existent. I chase the few scraps of his presence that exist online, reaching out to his clearly dusty Facebook account and getting nothing in return. I message his friends and either it's, "Sorry, I haven't seen him," or no reply at all. Andre has an arrest record, but it's minor stuff like driving without a license. A pal who taught with me at Commerce saw him at a jazz festival years back but can't offer me anything else.

I've also looked for the witnesses. Jayden and Miguel were in the hall with Andre. I can still see them gathered around him when he complained about being boot-violated. I can't find anything on Jayden, but in a depressing turn, I discover that Miguel is in jail for conducting a home invasion with a samurai sword. I could try to find him there, but it doesn't feel right.

By this point, I've begun the book that is now in your hands.

As pages accumulate, it becomes clear that the book will not be able to land without Andre. It will just circle the runway until it runs out of fuel and crashes in the forest. No survivors will be found, and perhaps no one will even bother to look. Andre and I need to have another conversation about the coffee cup and boots. I have my story, not his. I was on one side of the object – the paper cup – and he was on the other. More than that, it was his open palm that converted the object into a prop.

A teacher I worked with at Commerce sent me a few emails for some of Andre's friends and one that might even be Andre's email. I write to Andre, telling him I'm working on a book, that I can pay him for his time, not use his real name. Then, I click send, and my message jets off into the ether. I get a bad feeling. It's as if I am trying to track Andre down – *which I am* – and it feels invasive – *which it is*. This feeling gets worse when nothing comes back in return. I try the other emails for Andre's friends, and it's the same: I get nothing. Andre must be out there wondering, "Why is this guy Coady bothering my friends, and what's he after?" The more time passes, the more nothingness piles up, and the more nervous I get. The silence gets loud. It says things like, "Coady, that's the teacher that screwed me up for life," or, "What's wrong with this old guy? What does he want?"

Now, across from the house that is Andre's last known residence, I finally have a shot at making my case in person. I'm willing to wait it out like I'm on a stakeout, and I practice my speech to Whalen: *Hi, Andre, I don't know if you remember me, but I taught history at Commerce. I've been trying to track you down-*

Whalen interrupts. "Don't say, 'track him down.' Say you've been trying to find him. Maybe just start by saying, 'Remember me?'"

"Sure thing. He opens the door and I say, 'Remember me!?' I might as well go and punch myself in the face. I didn't expect to be this nervous," I tell Whalen.

"Well," he says, "You hit his foot. *Twice.*"

Ten years ago, I protest. Anyway, he doused me in hot coffee.

Whalen says, "So, maybe he's the nervous one."

What? How can he be nervous? He doesn't even know I'm down here. And you know, to be honest, that's actually part of *why* I'm nervous. I'm going to go over there, and he's going to be like, "What the hell is going on? How come my teacher from ten years ago is on my porch asking if I remember something that happened in a hallway a lifetime ago at Commerce?" I mean, if it was me, I'd be totally confused by all of it. I might even go blank. Or get mad.

"What are you worried about?" asks Whalen.

"I don't know – maybe he'll smack something out of my hands again, only this time I'm not holding anything. I hold up my empty hands."

Whalen helpfully picks up a coffee cup from the console. "Here, take this."

"Always the joker," I grumble.

"What are you *really* worried about?" asks Whalen.

"Me? Honestly? For real? I'm worried he's not going to remember a thing. Nada. Zip. Here I've spent hours traveling, got the beginning of a book rattling around in my head, and I've been marinating on this moment from ten years ago. I can see it so clearly, but what do I know? I don't care if he's mad at me. I wouldn't even mind it if he took a swing at me. I'm more worried he won't care or can't remember. It was years ago, and he was young. It's just another piece of history gone missing like most of it. And if he doesn't remember, did it really happen? It'd be like running into Brutus on the run and asking him why he stabbed Caesar, and he gives you a blank look and says, 'Caesar *who*?'"

Well, maybe not quite like that.

"Are you going to do this?" asks Whalen.

"Yeah," I say. "I'm going to go do this."

It's a sunny and mild afternoon, and it's a nice enough block – some single-family homes, some multi-family ones. Down the street, kids are playing soccer behind a chain-link fence. It's around six, so people are coming home from work, dragging trash cans back in from the curb, and vacuuming their cars.

It's hard to know exactly how to tackle the house, which is Andre's last known residence. From the sidewalk, I see a front porch packed with stuff and a Beware of the Dog sign – cliché, really, though at least there's no snarling or barking to go along with it. I could swing around the side and climb up to the second-floor porch, but I don't know which unit supposedly contains Andre. So, I take a breath and enter the lower porch, beginning by ringing the lower bell and when that gets nothing, the upper one. I stand there for at least four minutes, periodically trying, and then I hear footsteps descending down the staircase. Sounds youthful.

I'm holding my breath when the door swings open. For a second, I think it might be him. He's the right age, mid-20s, African American. But it's not Andre. And this guy, who is friendly enough but a little confused, knows who Andre is, though only vaguely. He tells me "they" left a year ago. Mail comes for them from time to time, but there's no forwarding address. It's the same kind of conversation that's happened a million times before. Someone looking for someone else and finding a cold trail. I tell him Andre's a former student of mine. He says, "Okay," then, "Yeah, sorry, if I knew where he was, I'd tell you." I thank him and leave, head back to the Tacoma, and report my failure to Whalen.

"Why don't you ask around," he says. "See what you get."

A Hispanic guy next door on the second-floor porch tells me in broken English he's just there watching the place for his nephew. He has no clue what I'm after. A young woman on the first floor of that building can't help me either. She remembers Andre, but that's it. People move in and out all the time and, "Why are you looking for him, anyway?"

"He's a former student. Just trying to track him down. I mean, find him."

"Well, that's nice, I guess," she says. "Good luck."

. . .

THIRTY MINUTES LATER, Whalen and I are having dinner at The Student Prince, one of the last good German restaurants in America. I've got the schnitzel, and he's got the sausage; there's an impaled pretzel swinging between us on a hook and two steins of Paulaners sweating it out on the table.

"What if you can't find him?" asks Whalen.

"I don't know, maybe I can write around it. I mean, this is part of history, too – people get lost, you can't find witnesses. You know what they say, history is written by the victors. And if I can't find him, no one can dispute my version."

Whalen shrugs. "Your version makes you look bad enough, anyway."

"True. So, maybe I should write a version in which Andre has the coffee cup, and I'm the one who is violated. Andre comes up to me and taps my boots twice."

"Okay, then what?" says Whalen.

"Then, I think about smacking the coffee cup out of his hand, only I don't. It becomes a lesson about restraint and goes on to change both of our lives."

"Boring," snorts Whalen.

Yeah, boring. If history ran smoothly, it wouldn't exist. It's only the backfires, the unexpected turns, that keep our attention. Would we know Caesar's name if he had ruled in perpetuity and died of natural causes? Besides, I'm not really a nihilist. I don't believe you can really stick to the facts, but I'd like to keep them close.

I say, "If I can't find Andre, I'll just offer my side of the story."

"Not ideal, though," says Whalen.

"No, not ideal. But what is?"

"It's a good story," says Whalen, "but you'll have to find him."

I drive back to Rhode Island, doing my best to stay alert and watch for deer on the highway. Because deer kill more Americans than sharks. Way more. Up to 200 Americans die every year because of deer. In comparison, one American dies every two years on account of sharks. But no scary movies are made about the danger of deer crossing the street. A century from now historians will study our national obsession with sharks, knowing nothing about deer, except maybe Lyme Disease. But barreling down to Rhode Island at 80 mph, encased in two tons of Detroit steel, I'm much more likely to leave Planet Earth after colliding with a deer than being down on the beach in Rhode Island and getting attacked by a shark. And I know this, but it doesn't slow me down. I just try to stay alert.

I get back around midnight and take a walk down to the beach. I look at the dark ocean and think, "There's probably a shark out there somewhere," but I'm safe on the land. A few days later, I'm in the air on a plane to Morocco, looking down at the ocean, wondering about sharks again. My conversation with Andre will have to wait.

Or perhaps it is not meant to be.

Maybe I'm okay with that. Maybe that's what I want.

. . .

BECAUSE THE PAPER cup has already served its purpose, right? There's no need to hear from Andre or track anyone else down. We're good here; the book is almost over. Sure, if I found him, we would learn more, we would get his side, see if he even remembers the moment, and that's cool.

But maybe, just maybe, the paper cup has been a different kind of prop all along. It's been a carrot to keep us moving through this book, or if we want to get crafty, the (prop)ulsion that has led us through more difficult terrain. Maybe there were moments in the backwoods of the Ohio Valley, or the fray of Revolutionary Paris, when we thought to ourselves, "This is good enough, interesting, but it's also kind of dense, and I don't see where Coady is taking all of this," but then we remembered Andre, the hallway, the paper cup, the promise of finding out what happened, and that helped to propel us forward.

We want to find out how stories end. We hang in there. And if we are the center of the story, which nearly all our leading characters are, we cling to the center and stay in the hunt by being the story. If everyone can't stop talking about Caesar, even when he fumbles a diadem, then they're not talking about anyone else. The story is Caesar; Caesar is the story. No one else can clamber up on stage unless they're on bended knee. Even in death, Caesar is the story, actors strutting around with beeswax likenesses of the man as torchlight flickers on their otherworldly faces.

Speaking of torches, Luther knows how to keep the story going and the people in their seats. He has a flair for the cliffhanger. He knows how to make a grand gesture, real or imagined. He may or may not have walked up to a church door and actually nailed 95 theses to it, but everyone seems to think he did, and that's a good story and good enough.

What good would Robespierre and Lenin have been to anyone if they entertained a single doubt about the certainty of where the story of mankind was ultimately heading? They would have been historical roadkill. You would not even know their names. Their stories had them erecting plaster mountains and using chalk to determine national borders on a moving train. One takes an army of carpenters to erect, the other a mere flick of the wrist, but they are both massive abstractions, equally captivating in their absurdities. They interest us still. We can't shake them despite the fact that they killed innocents by the boatload.

In the end, Chamberlain's biggest mistake is not sticking to his own story. We're always advised to accept our mistakes. Voters want to hear politicians apologize, but God forbid they get what they ask for. Out comes the cross, the hammers, the nails. Had old Neville stuck to his guns, even in the face of blitzkrieg, he would have attracted a following for the simple fact that people like to follow things. Some people thrive off contrarian viewpoints, don't like big crowds, and distinguish themselves by being apart from the mainstream.

Neville could have unapologetically whipped his umbrella around in public and made it clear that it was the failures of the prior generation, including his annoying half-brother Austen, the one with the bust in the National Gallery and the hoity-toity knighthood. You want to see a ridiculous piece of diplomacy? Check out Austen's Locarno Pact – total rubbish that paved the way to Munich much more than Neville's umbrella. But we don't know that because Chamberlain abandoned his story, abdicated his power, conceded his fault, and died in a bed listening to bombs drop nearby.

Neville should have studied George Washington, who mangled the truth beyond recognition but stuck to his story and survived Fort Necessity, later pulling off the founding of the American nation. You wouldn't find old GW equivocating or conceding a point. Because if you can't survive, you're useless. History is finished with you.

This book, like history, is a game of survival. If it is not known, it cannot be true. For all you know, the story with Andre and the paper cup might be entirely fabricated, just a narrative thread invented for the book to keep you reading. The kind of person who might do that to a reader is the same kind of person who would double step on a teenager's boots to see what might happen.

And so where does that leave us? Is Coady really messing with us again?

If this is the paperback copy, you might squeeze the book a bit tighter to gauge how many pages are left, and whether it is conceivable, based on that girth, that we will meet Andre again. If it's an e-book reader, you might look at the bottom right and check what percentage is left of the book, and again, question if there's time to meet Andre again.

Will we? Will we meet Andre again?

Life takes over once we're back in Morocco, including a late-night earthquake that sends us out on the street for the night. Mostly, I'm back in the hallway of a school again, only this hallway is concrete and the hot desert air pours in. There's plenty of play boxing with students, but here, I'm careful not to step on anyone's feet. By day, I teach Caesar, Luther, Robespierre, and Lenin. By night, I find a cafe, work on this book, and write about Caesar, Luther, Robespierre, and Lenin. Moped smoke and an occasional sandstorm blow through, and every once in a while, an aftershock gently nudges the bed.

I haven't forgotten about Andre, but I haven't done much more to find him, poking at a few remaining leads as if they're a cold plate of mashed potatoes. After writing *Paper Cup, Part 2*, I realized that having a conversation with Andre is basically essential. I acquire a confidential report on him. There's a real cell phone number there and an email, but I get nothing when I reach out, which only adds to my apprehension. By now, I'm convinced Andre wants nothing to do with me.

His dad's number is on the report, and somehow, I feel like this gives me a fighting chance. But I ignore that lead for more than a month. Not ready. Then, one Sunday night, with nothing in my way, and nothing to lose, I text Andre's father.

The response is immediate, as he tries to call me, only I'm not in America. It's a Google Voice number, and he texts me and wants to know why I don't have a real number. I'm trying to figure out a way to explain that when, in a bizarre coincidence of good cosmic timing, a text from a different number pops up on my phone: **Is this Cody?**

ME: Yes, this is Coady. Is this Andre?
ANDRE: Yes
ME: Great. How are you?
ANDRE: Good hbu

He goes quiet for a while, and it unnerves me. I'm surprised to be suddenly hearing from him after all my false starts, and now, I'm suspicious. We're each sniffing each other out. Here I am in Morocco having doubts about a text I'm getting – there he is in Springfield, probably having doubts about a text he's sending. Maybe Andre's dad, having tried to call me, is suspicious and tells Andre to be careful. You can't be sure who you're talking to. And he's right. Maybe Andre is on the other end of the phone; maybe he's slipping away.

I text him to say I can pay him for his time, and he texts back:

ANDRE: Word?

I'm pretty sure I know what this means, but I go find my wife and ask, "What does 'Word?' mean? It's Andre. I'm texting with him."

She, of course, knows all about Andre.

"Andre? You're texting with Andre? Coffee cup Andre?"

"Yes, I told him I could pay for his time, and he wrote back, 'Word?'"

My wife looks at me like I'm an idiot. "Word? It means, like, *really*? It's good. He's in."

Okay, he's in. That's what I thought.

Andre and I go back and forth, spending most of two hours trying to connect our electronic nerve endings. This includes but is not limited to, him downloading Zoom, him checking to see if his PayPal account is active, me trying to get Apple Pay going, him trying to get into his email to get the Zoom link, me trying to download Cash App, me sitting on my couch in Marrakech, wondering if this is really Andre I'm texting and if it's going to work. There's one particularly painful stretch of 20 minutes when he needs to update his phone or grant permissions or something else, and I feel like he's slipping away.

Then, his name pops up on Zoom, and I let him into the "room."

HE'S IN HIS CAR, parked, and the phone is pointing up from his lap. He has a winter hat on. So, it's hard to tell for sure whether it is Andre or not.

I ask him if he remembers me.

"Yup, I remember you. I spoke with you at an agency, a job agency."

My heart sinks. "No," I tell him. "I taught you at Commerce."

"Yup, I remember you from Commerce. But you look just like this dude who worked at this agency. I thought it was you, anyway."

My plan has always been to cut to the chase – to get him as fresh as possible. I ask him if he remembers something that happened in the hallways one morning when we were at Commerce – something that was a real episode.

He thinks about it, kind of the way he thought about when I stepped on his foot a second time. He seems to be considering his options like there's something inside his mind waiting to get out, but he's not sure if he should let it. And now, I'm sure it's Andre because of that look in his eyes. It's just like the look he had when we were standing in the hall years ago, facing off over a paper cup filled with hot coffee. He's calculating, wondering where the conversation is going, what he's supposed to say, and if he should follow through.

"You talking about the thing with the coffee?" he finally says.

We both laugh. More than ten years have passed, and we're right back where it all began, both of us thinking about the linoleum and the hall and the packs of kids before school starts. He's with his friends again, and I have the coffee cup as he is about to approach throwing mock punches.

I say, "Andre, what was going on from your point of view? What happened?"

"Well, I remember I didn't know if you were playing or not. But you stepped on my boot, and I was like, 'Don't do it again.' And then you did it again. And that's when I spilled coffee on you."

Spilled is something of an understatement, but I don't point that out. I remind him that he came up to me. We were play boxing, just fooling around.

He interrupts, "You were my favorite teacher, though."

I'm flattered and surprised. Because I didn't actually know if kids like Andre – kids who consistently tested their teachers and pushed the boundaries and broke rules – had favorite teachers. I let him know that I liked him, too. That he was a funny guy, and that I felt like we were always testing one another.

"Yup, yup," he nods.

"Andre, when I stepped on your foot the first time, the next thing I knew you were back with your friends. Do you remember what you said to them?"

"That, I don't remember."

Because I heard you say, 'Coady, just stepped on my boot!'

"Yup, yup, yup," he says.

"And I was over here, like ten feet away, and I was like, 'He's just joking.' So, I thought okay, I'm going to go up to him. And I went up to you, and that's when I stepped on your boot again. What did you think at that moment?"

"At that point, I thought you were a gangster teacher." He laughs. "I knew you weren't like any other teacher. Like you wouldn't get stepped on. I was kind of testing your energy, too. I was trying to see what kind of relationship we could have in the future. Because I thought you were cool. Honestly.

I was just like damn, he just stepped on my foot again. He really is a gangster teacher."

"And that's when you slapped my coffee. Why?"

He thinks about this. "I just wanted to be fear, I guess."

"Do you remember the reaction of the other kids?"

"They were pretty surprised, I think. They were like, 'Yo! What happened with you all? Damn! You just spilled coffee all over him!' And I was like, 'But he just stepped on my shoe!' It was funny, I'm not going to lie."

"And did you think you were in trouble? The bell rang and you went into math class. Were you in there thinking you were in trouble?"

"To be honest, I didn't know it was that serious. But the other kids in class, they were like, 'Yo, what happened?'"

"So, you didn't think, 'This is gonna come back on me?'"

"I didn't think it was that serious because of what we did to each other. I had an idea I might get in trouble, but probably not right away, because yo, that's how Commerce was. You'd get in trouble two weeks later. But that time, two seconds later, in comes Coach Harris and he's like 'Come with me' and I'm like, 'Whoa!'"

Andre is right. It was fast for Commerce; though, it probably took more like ten minutes for Coach Harris, the hulking Dean of the School, to get Andre out of class and bring him to where Principal Davis and I had set up in my own room. Three big adults, three big authorities, one young student, one Andre.

But Andre reminds me of something I had forgotten.

"You apologized first. That's how it started."

I remember that now. Andre sat down and I said, "Look, I'm sorry," and then told him why. I explained I wasn't exactly sure why I did that, tapping his boot, but it was wrong. Things eased up from there, and we could talk more freely. What did we say?

"I don't really remember what else exactly," says Andre. "But I remember what I learned. It was about emotions. Like, anything that's not about my life, don't take it too seriously. If it's not a big deal, just let it go. It's not worth getting hurt over. Honestly, I think I was going through it that day."

"Yeah," I say, "You'd been running with a rough crowd."

"Jayden. Remember Jayden?" he says. "He was there that day. I think he's the one I told you stepped on my boot. You know he's dead?"

I did not.

"Yup," says Andre, "car crash."

We talk about Mateo, who is in jail. Armando, who ran at a cop with a knife, is now dead as well. Miguel is in prison following an ill-advised home invasion with a samurai sword.

I ask Andre about his mom, and he lights up.

I tell him that she really made an impression on me.

"Yup," he nods. Then, out of the blue, he says, "We was both wrong,"

"Maybe, Andre, but I was wrong first."

"We was both wrong," he repeats.

He tells me he's a delivery driver for Domino's now. He'll drive for DoorDash when the background check comes back.

He's still figuring out what to do with his life. I tell him he's smart and funny; he'll figure it out.

"Andre, I'll send you the chapter and then we can talk after that."

"Sounds good, let's do that."

"We'll talk again in a week."

"Yup, sounds good."

It's good we have a plan because, once we close out of the Zoom call, I realize something: I still have one more question for him. And it's a big one.

I REACH out to Andre again in a week. We set up a time to meet – 9 pm my time, Morocco, 3 pm his time, Springfield. But when he clicks on the Zoom link, we're connected for only a few words before he vanishes. He gets back on, another few words, and he is gone again. Ah, technology.

It is like before, the both of us reaching around the curvature of planet Earth trying to intertwine on electronic nerve endings, but this time, it's not working so well. He texts me that his phone has no service, and I tell him we can text back and forth if he likes. It's kind of a cop-out on my part and maybe his too. I'm aware that the texting might lead to the exchange lacking gravitas and intimacy. But in that, as with many things regarding Andre and a paper cup filled with hot coffee, I am wrong.

I have, of course, my big question lined up, but I pepper him with a few smaller ones to warm up. I ask him when he left Commerce. I'm looking for a date but Andre texts back: **After I got expelled.** He tells me it was for selling weed, and it was tough because he at least wanted to try to graduate. When I ask him about the building, and what it was like, he either doesn't understand the question or is just avoiding it, texting back: **I enjoyed my time there cause I got to learn a lot of things.**

Honestly, this text seems like something you'd tell a teacher because it's what a teacher would like to hear. So, I abandon the pleasantries and jump to the question that is really on my mind, texting: **When I stepped on your boot the second time you were obviously mad, which I get. And I understand you had to show your friend that you weren't going to allow that. If I hadn't been holding the coffee cup, do you think you would have hit me instead of hitting the coffee cup?**

He doesn't take long this time. It's only a minute, and when the text pops up on my laptop, it lands like a brick tossed through my window: **That's a good question but my answer to that is anonymous cause it didn't happen so that would be non existence.** It sounds like a piece of French deconstructionist philosophy, but I get what he's saying immediately: he won't go there. He can see why it might be interesting to speculate, but he won't. Perhaps it's too dangerous. Maybe he can't afford those kinds of musings. Life is too immediate. Andre's contrafactual is *what if* he graduated Commerce. My *what if* is what would have happened if I hadn't so tactically covered my ass that day.

Of course, an alternative explanation is that Andre is at peace with his choice. He was faced with a challenge that threatened his prestige and social standing, coming from a person who held massive institutional authority and backing. He could have really reacted and taken a shot at me. Instead, he calculated his response more carefully and went after a suitable proxy, the paper cup.

Despite my advice to avoid conflict at all costs, Andre may actually have saved us both a major headache by taking a swipe at the paper cup. The entire episode lasted no more than 60 minutes from start to finish, something you could catch on Netflix. It began as he moved toward me through play punches and ended with me walking him back to math class. And we finished out the year together, we had some laughs, and now, ten years later, we are still talking about it. Machiavelli would have been proud.

Still, I'd like to imagine what would have happened without the paper cup. Seeking clarity, and holding out hope he might still follow me into the contrafactual void and give me more words to add to this book in your hand, I text: **Ok, so you're saying there's no way we can know?** But no, he won't follow me there. He texts: **I'm saying it didn't exist so my answer to that is anonymous because it didn't happen in reality which means that it wasn't real.**

He's consistent and clear, and there's an authority to that. I have to accept it. But there's just one more thing I want to know. I text: **But let me ask you, when I hit your boot the** second time, were you really angry at me? Or was it more like you didn't want to let that stand?

He doesn't answer the question directly.

He texts: **It was about respect.**

Then he texts: **That's how I grew up.**

We've defined the word "props" here, in the simplest sense, as being short for property, an object used in a theatrical or film performance, like a gun or a well-worn couch. This book has been a meditation on what it means to have a prop outside of this theatrical world, in history, so-called real life, or what Andre might call existence. But there's another meaning for the word props, and while it is more recent, or because of that, it is actually used a lot more frequently.

According to Urbandictionary.com, "props" is a *"Slang term for 'accolades,' 'proper respect,' or 'just dues.' Popularized in the 1980s by rappers who shortened the term 'propers' which was in turn being used as an abbreviated version of "proper respect" at least by the 1960s. The increase in this term's usage during the late 1980s and early 1990s coincided with an increasing fascination with the mafia within rap circles. Both communities have traditionally placed great emphasis on the importance of earning and giving respect."*

Although each chapter has had its object prop, a case can be made that this book has actually been about the respect version of "props" all along – or, put another way, that feeling of submission, or at least acceptance, for someone else being excellent and in charge. Because that is society in a nutshell. We always need, one way or another, to figure out who is going to be in charge. It may be with a sharp blade, it may be with a piece of chalk, but conditions must conspire, and personalities must exert themselves to create order out of our chaos.

An object, something with bling, like a diadem or a belt of wampum, might connotate "props" of this kind, but in fact, it is secondary to the fact that it must be received. They represent the respect that you earn. Props of this kind cannot be bought like the friendship beads I lined my shirt with in the 5th grade only to remove in the face of scrutiny. Props must be given to you. Caesar might have known this, enlisting Mark Antony to do the dirty work, but it didn't work because it was not truly earned, at least not according to the denizens of Rome. Chamberlain, on the other hand, might have done well to reconsider the props he so readily handed over to the Fuhrer.

In our first conversation about the event, Andre said he came toward me play boxing because he wanted to see what kind of future we could have. A second knock on a boot and a slap of a coffee cup followed, all quietly and quickly contained, but now it is more than ten years later, and we're still talking, reaching out halfway around the world. If he had not come at me that morning, if I had not erred in striking his boot a second time, if he had not reacted by slapping the cup out of my hands, we would likely have had no future, and this conversation would never have taken place. Because history is mostly the study of mistakes, backfires, and the carelessness of people. Without the episode, Andre would just be one of thousands of students I let loose upon the world never to be seen again, and I would have just been some teacher he could barely remember. He was trying to see if we had a future, and in a convoluted combination of accidental and purposeful events, we did.

He also used the word anonymous when I asked him to reimagine what might have happened if the paper cup had not been there. He said it was "anonymous cause it didn't happen so that would be non existence."

You might remember that this is how I described the High School of Commerce in the first chapter, a hulking mass of anonymous hallways that all looked the same in a building designed to keep its occupants completely concealed from the outside world. If you were a brand-new student, or the brand-new teacher placed there to receive the brand-new students, it was a Fortress of Obscurity, an easy place to get lost, both emotionally and spiritually.

In a way, this book has been a rescue mission. I've enlisted some of the heavies of history – regardless of their own willingness – to aid me as I've descended back in time, a rope tied around my waist, through my own history to pluck Andre and myself, out of the anonymity of the fourth floor of the High School of Commerce. Glory may be fleeting, as Napoleon supposedly said, but obscurity is forever. And while the encounter between Andre and me that winter morning may fall short of being truly glorious, we are now, at least, free from total obscurity.

Hopefully, by now, you know a bit about Andre, even though that is not his real name. You can see, as I can, that he was awake back then, making dozens of decisions every morning. He was presented with an unexpected, complicated situation, and he made choices to preserve his position, which forced me to make my own choices to maintain my own position.

An immense amount of energy went into that one moment – all the crushing weight of American Society, circa 2014. Dozens upon dozens of environmental conditions, social cues, and sad truths were redirected onto a lonely paper cup filled with hot coffee. Instead of becoming a major event in our lives, it remained a contained one, though memorable for both of us. For me, the story has been built up over the years into a living history; now, in this book, it has been constructed, built up, torn down, and reconstructed as a piece of written history.

In the end, this book is an attempt to correct a mistake of mine from long ago. Because when Andre came at me that winter morning, on the fourth floor of the High School of Commerce, throwing play punches he was already giving me props, or my "just propers." He was letting me know I wasn't just any teacher, that I could hang, that I was cool, and that we might even have a future. And I must have felt that, wanted more, and used the tool that has always been at my disposal – humor – to try to get more. And that was where the door between us slammed shut. But now, years later, this book has pried it open again. That's great, and I'm glad about the way things worked out, but the truth remains: that winter morning in the hall on the fourth floor, I failed to give Andre the respect he deserved.

So now, "Andre," here it is, finally, lying open in your hands, the same hands that smacked away the hot cup of coffee of mine and have now found themselves in the future. I hope you see yourself here, in this book, and see that I see you here, and hopefully, others see you as you were: funny, daring, shrewd, and capable, which is why this book is dedicated to you.

I'm giving you the *Props* you deserve.

AFTERWORD
FEBRUARY 15TH, 2024

Before I proceed with an outpouring of thanks, I'd like to make a request: if you enjoyed this book, I'd be grateful if you were able to give it a good review — or talk about it incessantly with friends and families. If you bought the paperback, lend it to a friend. And remember, talking knowledgeably about history makes you look attractive, so you might also want to discuss *Props* on your social media platforms and dating apps – again, incessantly.

If this book was published by a publishing house you would not be reading these words. But it is not. It is self-published, and I'm not too proud to ask for your support. Do you know why people starting out are always saying getting reviews is essential? *Because getting good reviews is essential.* Folks, I'm waging war with Tik Tok on one side, A.I. on the other. Do me a favor: review this book – talk incessantly about it – get a tattoo of the cover on your bicep.

I would be so grateful.

This book has been a transatlantic affair, begun in the humid summer of Matunuck, Rhode Island, and completed in the dry winter air of Marrakech, Morocco. Early stages were hammered out in air-conditioned reading rooms of the South Kingston Public Library; final touches were applied poolside at the Club Des Pharmaciens under a steady sun and a cold breeze. *Props* has been a constant companion – or an animal needing to be tamed – depending on the day. An assortment of objects auditioned for roles in this book. What you have in your hands are, to my best understanding, those deserving to be scattered across our stage.

Take a bow, *Props*.

It could be easy to see this book as a fairly wide-ranging affair, a trip 2,000 years into the past and back, yet my own family seems to keep finding its way to a nature documentary narrated by Morgan Freeman and detailing the gaseous formation of planet earth and its periodic (separated by hundreds of millions of years) mass extinctions. Whoa: *perspective*. As the great singer David St. Hubbins once said, "Too much f%$&ing perspective." It might send you into an existential tailspin, or it may give you comfort. Whatever the case, the space between you and a bleeding-out Caesar on a Senate floor is imperceptible by comparison. Taking the long view, we're all the same being, and 2,000 years isn't even the blink of an eye. So, give up, and live it up.

As punchy and glib as this book is, it does have its roots in actual historical sources. A score of excellent books and many more scholarly articles informed my understanding. I'm not sure if these historians would show up to collect their door prizes but here goes.

My chapter on Caesar was greatly aided by the excellent *The Death of Caesar* by Barry Strauss and *The Assassination of Caesar: A People's History of Rome* by Michael Parenti.

I am in debt to the 2003 film *Luther*. Not only have you entertained and educated my students, allowing me a two-block break in class every year, you have forced me to go deeper and locate that lovable loser, Andreas Karlstadt. It did not lead to an Illuminati hunting trip to Wittenberg, but I did crack open *Frederick the Wise. Seen and Unseen Lives of Martin Luther's Protector* by Sam Wellman. I also maxed out my Jstor.org account, harvesting the riches therein. A special shout-out goes to the article *Andreas Bodenstein von Karlstadt and Martin Luther: It's Complicated* by Stryder Matthews. Honestly, it's not easy to make sense of this mess we call history, so thanks for trying.

Paul R. Misencik's *George Washington and the Half-King Chief Tanacharison* is an admirable book. For one, it's lean and compelling. But I also think it's heartening that it comes from a historical self-starter, working closely with his wife, Sally. The book is a real contribution to the life of our first president and brings the Half King into focus. If anyone's interested, there are plenty of interesting articles about wampum out there. Try *The Functions of Wampum* by George S. Snyderman if you want to get your toes wet. Written in 1954, it's a little dated but even that aspect makes it a worthy curiosity.

Colin Jones' *Fall of Robespierre, Fatal Purity* by Ruth and Jonathan Smyth's *Robespierre's and the Festival of the Supreme Being* gave insight into, and sometimes compassion for, the madman Maximilien Robespierre. As I mentioned in the *Papier Mâché* chapter, a couple of historians actually responded to my email queries. I find it heartening that experts in their field would field and reply to questions from a freelance writer with no academic credentials. Thanks to Hervé Leuwers and Colin Jones for their assistance.

Catherine Merridale's *Lenin on the Train* is a fun read about a difficult man. The *April Theses* are a difficult read by a difficult man – penned, in part, on a difficult train ride. If you're willing to navigate the questionable maze of Marxist writing, there's plenty else out there about Lenin and his train ride. You may not find the German gold, but you'll have a good time trying.

Thanks, I guess, go to John Fitzgerald Kennedy for his book *Why England Slept*. It feels a little awkward thanking a deceased president, but there you go. If nothing else, Jack, you attempted to come to the aid of Neville Chamberlain, something he was unwilling to do himself. You may have been greatly aided by your powerful father, but the light of your ambition belonged to you, even when it was only flickering. Thanks also go to all the Kennedy assassination theorist freaks out there for making the congressional testimony of Louie Steven Witt so easily accessible. A debt of gratitude is also owed to Witt himself for providing such an odd moment – every day you went for a walk at lunch, and only one sunny day you brought your umbrella. The rest is history – or, in your case, another page in a sheaf of false positives.

There's an endless list of writers who have informed my own attempt here, but during the creation of this book, one stood out for me: Frank McCourt. When I was training to be a teacher at the advanced age of 38, I read his book, *Teacher Man*, and thought, "That's it! That's how I want to teach!" I never kicked a student's feet out from under him, slamming them to the ground (makes my transgression with Andre's boots look quite tame by comparison), but a lot of the other spontaneous pedagogy has worked its way into my routines.

While this next passage risks sounding like an Oscar speech that cannot be contained, there are a lot of people I would like to thank just for being part of my life. A big shout-out to all our people at Roy Carpenter's Beach in Matunuck. It is a piece of living history and a piece of paradise. Up on our Eastside hill, we enjoy the protection of the ruling dynasties – the Fergusons, the Shalveys, the Hannons, the Contis – and appreciate our adopted grandparents, Bob and Nancy, as well as our dear kinfolk holding the line on the seaside: Scott, Lolita, and all the awesome Roberts. We are also proud to keep company with select Westside allies: the Lebrun-Giards. Peace is hard to achieve, but our coexistence across the tense geopolitical divides of Roy's is proof that it is possible.

Much thanks and love also goes to John Johnson and

Susan Short for all the support they have given me over the years. It's more than just patronage or friendship; it's family.

Marrakech is such a special place, wild & free. We have been so blessed to fall into a community here, both at the school and at the residency, Nakhil III. The Portuguese, the French, the Brits, the Brazilians, the Irish, the Koreans, the Mexicans, the Moroccans, our fellow Americans – you all know who you are. Can you hear the shouts coming from the courtyard, our little village in action?

Our time in the Kech has also been made special by excellent hosts. Laura and Hicham, among many other things, you gave us the best-tasting Thanksgiving feast outside of the States — or inside. Priti, we're so grateful to you and all the positive energy you've brought to our lives. You chose to organize the holiday bazaar but could easily run a major industrialized nation.

I'm grateful for all my colleagues at ASM, past and present. Like Morocco, nothing always works at the school but everything works out. Along with my other amazing colleagues, I'd like to give a special thanks to department chief Mackenzie Young, who laid down enough cover fire to allow for an army of mules to make it to Moscow unscathed. Here's to hoping we'll serve in the same trenches sometime again soon.

Stateside, thanks go to Mike Chapedlaine for getting me the report that led to me "Andre." Thanks to O'Donnell for moral support. Whalen, thank you for spending an afternoon wandering around Springfield; I can always count on you to be game. Thank you, Danny DeCillis, for your wise and constructive developmental and line edits – you're a kind and informative voice. Thanks to Kelsey Yurek for working with me and hanging on during the proofing stage. Thanks to Zack Hacker, a bit of stateside here in Marrakech, for helping me push this book out into the world. I'm hoping our collaboration will continue, perhaps with a history book of your own.

Of course, thanks go to "Andre" for knocking the paper cup out of my hand, being able to find your way out of the bind I presented you, and coming to peace with me to finish out your 9th-grade year. It's been such a pleasure to speak with you now in your adult life. You're a survivor, and for me, as a history teacher, there is no higher form of praise.

Thank you, students from the past, present, and future. Had someone informed me when I was young that I'd find myself back in high school for most of my years, I would have punched them in the face. My grief and rage would have been deep and abiding. But now I'm pretty sure it's the best job in the world – making it all up as I go along, surrounded by teenagers – the funniest, most alive, most open people on Planet Earth. We've forgiven each other our shortcomings, moved on, and taken on new terrain, which is a good name for a band. Should I put it up on the wall? No, you're right. Not that one.

Thanks to my families: the one I grew up with, the one I married into, and the one I co-founded. Robyn's family is such a vivid assortment of personalities – witty, capable, ambitious, and headstrong. It's an honor to be part of the clan. Thanks to my brother and sister, who have been on the earthly journey with me from day one. Thanks to my father, who has long since passed but would have loved the intentions of this book. Thank you, Mom; there's no way I can ever repay the constant care you put in me, but I can try to pass it along to those in my charge, Harper and Rockwell. I see you in them, and for that, above all else, I have faith. The two of them have watched Dad get mixed up in one historical wrestling match after another. Thanks for being in my corner, kids. I'll always be in yours.

Thank you, Robyn. We began this life as strangers, and now, all these years later, we have this little universe we preside over. It's not always easy, but it's always meaningful, and it gets deeper and more considered as time passes. I trust you as an artist and a fellow writer. You dole out plenty of pills I need to swallow. Thank you for being honest.

To finish, I'm including an obituary I wrote for Mr. (Dr.) Lilien, my own high school history teacher who set me on a path into the profession. Mr. Lilien, I hope you are reading this book wherever you are now – *above*, most definitely *above* – and recognize your own teaching in these pages. Yes, you might even call it a kind of plagiarism. If you were still on Earth, you would be able to use your dormant law degree to bring suit against me, but I doubt you would. More likely, you'd give me a long, knowing look and be done with it. In any event, in case you're curious about what I thought of you (and so many others), here it is...

Afterword

Word on the street is that Mr. Lilien has passed away. For me, he was a hero. Mr. Lilien and Mr. Cleary shone in the firmament of the Concord Carlisle history department as twin stars. They were so remarkable that any argument on who was better would quickly be cut short with an understanding that they were both magnificent and to compare the two was to dissolve their shared magic. It was almost sacred.

He taught European history. If the building was still there, I could take you right to my seat. He leaned into his lesson like a boxer, wielding the Socratic method like a teamster, gesticulating like Vladimir Lenin, his wit sharp, his love evident, his target clear. At the age of 17, nothing was more important than to be able to answer one of Mr. Lilien's questions and have him reel back in amazement and recognition. And what he conjured with his passion was a bond between the students. We loved Mr. Lilien because he made us love one another, to feel as if we were hot on the heels of the truth, ready once and for all to bag and zip-tie it. There were nights in my 1982 Toyota Celica (the 4-wheel, 4-cylinder love of my life) spinning around a rotary on the way to Harvard Square, Wagner pumped up at maximum volume, and my friends and I would spontaneously chant, "LIL-I-EN! LIL-I-EN! LIL-I-EN!" Did he know that he inspired that level of devotion?

When I met my wife and decided to begin a life with her, I deduced the need to find a sustaining profession. We were on the couch in her Brooklyn apartment when she informed me her grandmother had reservations about my bohemian lifestyle. I offered, "Well, I guess if I could be anyone, I'd be Mr. Lilien," a proclamation that sent me on a whirlwind tour of degrees, student teaching stints, certifications, hard days, and small triumphs. Some days, at the end of the day, I might say to myself, with some awe, "Wow, I was like Lilien today." It was always the goal and still is.

Now, I teach history in Marrakech, Morocco. I am not Mr. Lilien every day, but even Mr. Lilien was not Mr. Lilien every day. He was a man who worked with what he was given, a graduate of Harvard Law School who'd dropped down to the middle path of teaching and a coach who built a high school fencing program into a regional powerhouse that took on M.I.T. and Brown. He was an intellect and an author who wrote "Water Is Rising in the Classroom," a compilation of teacher nightmares. I saw him once after leaving CCHS, and he told me he'd had a nightmare about me. I was there, right in my seat in the middle of the room, and I had a giant cyclops eye staring him down. You can only imagine how flattered I was.

Mr. Lilien taught us about the so-called great leaders of the 20th century with a wry understanding of their limitations but also their strengths. He brought me into an understanding of the past, almost a priesthood of a kind, the belief that the past can be absurd but important and that we all have to work with what we are given: like me, 17 years old, still awkward, often wayward, but questioning and eager to please. He gave me so much. Thank you, Mr. Lilien.

Matunuck, Rhode Island - Marrakech, Morocco
2023-2024

ABOUT THE AUTHOR

Norm Coady is a juggler and a thief. He has taught high school history on three continents, is a devoted Red Sox fan, and loves his family above all. He does his best to shape young minds by teaching stuff he barely understands.

Made in the USA
Middletown, DE
29 March 2024